Greening Your
HOSPITALITY
BUSINESS

For Accommodations, Tour Operators, and Restaurants

**Jill Doucette and
JC Scott**

Self-Counsel Press
(a division of)
International Self-Counsel Press Ltd.
USA   Canada

Self-Counsel Press acknowledges the financial support of the Government of Canada through the Canada Book Fund for our publishing activities.

Printed in Canada.

First edition: 2015

Library and Archives Canada Cataloguing in Publication

Doucette, Jill, 1986-, author
    Greening your hospitality business: for accommodations, tour operators, and restaurants / Jill Doucette and JC Scott.

Issued in print and electronic formats.
ISBN 978-1-77040-250-8 (paperback).—ISBN 978-1-77040-454-0 (epub).—ISBN 978-1-77040-455-7 (kindle)

    1. Hospitality industry—Environmental aspects. 2. Business enterprises—Environmental aspects. 3. Social responsibility of business. I. Scott, J. C., (John Cameron), author II. Title.

TX911.D69 2015	647.94	C2015-903700-X
		C2015-903701-8

Icons at the beginning of each chapter were designed by Travis Doucette and used with permission.

The Case Study for Holiday Park Resort in Chapter 7 was used with permission from Don Culic and Carolyn Robertson.

Self-Counsel Press
(a division of)
International Self-Counsel Press Ltd.

Bellingham, WA   North Vancouver, BC
        USA   Canada

Contents

Tables and Charts

Samples

Notice to Readers

Every effort is made to keep this publication as current as possible. However, the authors, the publisher, and the vendor of this book make no representations or warranties regarding the outcome or the use to which the information in this book is put and are not assuming any liability for any claims, losses, or damages arising out of the use of this book. The reader should not rely on the authors or the publisher of this book for any professional advice. Please be sure that you have the most recent edition.

Website links often expire or web pages move; at the time of this book's publication the links were current.

Introduction

Business is, without a doubt, one of the most powerful forces in society today. With the power and ability to influence our communities comes the vast potential to make a positive impact on the world. The hospitality sector is poised to be a change-maker within the realm of sustainability. Hospitality business have a particular ability to influence society for a few reasons:

- They are places where people congregate.
- They are major purchasers of goods and services.
- They typically have a high environmental impact per square foot, compared to other industries.
- They are keystones of our cultures and communities.
- They are often respected and trusted brands and can inspire businesses in other sectors.

By greening your hospitality company and taking action on areas such as alternative energy, waste reduction, sustainable purchasing, and community support, you will see a shift in your corporate culture. You will see new loyal clientele, a change in your environmental impact, and have the potential to influence other companies.

Whether your business is a restaurant, hotel, resort, clubhouse, cafeteria, or another hospitality business, this book will show you how going green can help the environment as well as your business. The planet needs leaders in sustainability, and that leadership does not go unrecognized. Customers want to see action, and they are starting to choose businesses with values that match their own.

The chapters in this book will give you practical information for greening your business with real examples of sustainability projects implemented in hotels and restaurants around the world.

1. The Business Case for Going Green

A recent global population study stated that numbers will continue to grow this century and the world will have "between 9.6 and 12.3 billion people in 2100."[1] Our lifestyles and many industries put enormous pressure on the planet. If the planet is to support 11 billion people in the near future, we need to change the way we live, work, and run our businesses to sustain and coexist with other species. Our natural wonders — the great ocean reefs, herds of grazing animals, lush tide pools, and clean rivers — are all at risk. Species in all habitats are in peril and we have already lost many due to human-induced changes to the environment.

The problems seem enormous but hope lies in the fact that we can make a difference, in the same way that real and meaningful change always begins, with small steps taken in the right direction. Businesses are starting to shift and the results are significant. We are now witnessing hotels that are completely "off the grid," and restaurants that are sourcing 100 percent seasonal and local produce. This environmental leadership is raising the bar across the hospitality sector.

According to the American Hotel & Lodging Association, in 2012 there were more than 50,000 hotel properties and almost 5 million guest rooms in the United States.[2] In Canada, in 2015, there were more than 8,000 properties and almost half a million rooms.[3] If every hotel in North America reduced energy and water consumption and tackled waste, the carbon footprint of the tourism sector would be drastically reduced.

Even more impressive is the number of restaurants worldwide — in the range of 7 to 12 million — but the industry changes quickly and

---

1 "World population stabilization unlikely this century," *Science*,
   accessed September 2015. www.sciencemag.org/content/346/6206/234
2 "2013 Lodging Industry Profile," American Hotel & Lodging Association,
   accessed September 2015. https://www.ahla.com/content.aspx?id=35603
3 "Hotel Industry Fact Sheet," Hotel Association of Canada, accessed September 2015.
   www.hotelassociation.ca/forms/Hotel%20Industry%20Facts%20Sheet.pdf

developing countries are rapidly expanding various food services, so no one is sure of the exact number; there could be 15 million.

Though the hospitality sector took a tough hit from 2008 to 2009, it has staged a strong rebound, and more growth means more environmental impact. Full-service dinner houses and fast food restaurants are all looking at ways to minimize environmental impact to reduce costs, maintain a positive public image, and reduce the risks of climate change. Take a look at Table 1 for information about relevant carbon emissions.

Table I
Carbon Emissions

	Carbon Emissions per Day
The average person's diet	7 kg CO_2e
Hotel rooms (mid-scale)	16.8 kg CO_2
Hotel rooms (upscale)	33.338 kg CO_2

Source: How We Calculate, Carbonfund.org, accessed October, 2015. www.carbonfund.org/how-we-calculate

Reducing environment impact in your business has great perks such as marketability, staff retention due to stronger corporate ethics, regulatory compliance, and financial benefits through eco-efficiencies. As few as five years ago, one could imagine that a hospitality business could plan for the future with only passing attention to sustainability principles; however, today with climate change at the forefront, and the millennial generation expecting responsible social and environmental behavior from the businesses they support or want to work for, green is a new imperative for business.

Consumers, particularly millennials, are not only shopping for *value*, they are shopping to see whether *your values are aligned with theirs*. By making choices such as shopping locally; promoting organics; and selecting regional wines, craft beers, and spirits, you can connect with a conscious clientele who understands the impact of their spending.

Embracing and adapting to change is what survival is all about. Green changes that are now normal in restaurants, hotels, resorts, and throughout the hospitality industry include recycling, water conservation, energy efficiency, and increased social responsibility. Do you see any of these going away? The issues of resource scarcity will persist, and therefore, we can expect the "green movement" to be not a trend, but a paradigm shift in commerce.

Change is a necessary constant in business and the ability to be opportunistic in the face of change can be a determining factor in a business's success or failure. Failure to see, accept, and plan for change is dangerous. One of the biggest forces for change in the food and beverage industry in the next decade is likely to be some form of reaction to climate change affecting our food supply and necessitating increasing environmental regulations.

Your business can start charting the course to reduce environmental impact. Change in any business must be planned for and budgeted. The planning process will allow those in your company to realize that a sustainability plan has numerous benefits. For example, many jurisdictions and utility companies still have early adopter grants and incentives that can assist your business with changing lighting, water fixtures, and installing alternative energy systems.

More radical changes that are entering the market include solar heating, geothermal energy, photovoltaic energy, recycled fryer oil running biodiesel vehicles, LED lighting, induction cooking, and many more innovations. There will be more, many of which we will discuss in the following chapters.

Over the past few years, we have surveyed owners of restaurants and hotels asking them if they were actively engaged in sustainability, and if the answer was yes, what their reasons were. The responses were surprising. Most said they were engaged in sustainability because of personal ethics, but others stated their reasons were marketing, winning contracts, employee retention, regulation, and cost savings. Also interesting to note is that the main reason for going green was ethics, but the main barrier was the cost. Therefore, it was important for owners to justify their sustainability program by gaining cost savings to pay for new sustainability initiatives.

1.1 Ethics

One of the first reasons that people go green is their ethics, which is defined as a moral duty and obligation to do "good" and to do the "right thing." Because people generally feel good about bringing their personal values into their places of work, corporate leaders in hospitality are steering their companies in a new direction. As our society learns more about global environmental issues, people in business are starting to find ways to mitigate environmental impact for the simple reason that they would like to do their part to protect the planet. Knowledge is a powerful motivator when it comes to ethical action. The increase in awareness of the state of our planet has motivated the doers of the world to take action and lead by example in their businesses.

Despite the fact that not everyone is personally committed to sustainable change, most people see it as the future. Consider where your business will be in five years. Will you and your customers be more conscious about energy and resource consumption? We expect that the entire hospitality industry will be greener and more efficient and also that the sector will be reaping benefits beyond simple cost savings from an engaged and supportive public.

1.2 Marketing

The second strong driver in the growing green movement is marketing, because sustainability is a new deciding factor for a growing segment of consumers. There has been impressive growth in the green sector of the economy even in the aftermath of the 2008 meltdown. As the economy continues to recover, one can expect even faster growth throughout the green sector. Consumers today are seeking more sustainable products and services; they are looking for healthier food alternatives, higher quality products, local businesses, and many are interested in spending in ways that preserve the environment.

When a business is seen to "walk its talk," it builds consumer confidence. People are skeptical of greenwashing claims (i.e., companies that spend time and money claiming to be "green" but don't actually implement green practices) so credible marketing and communication is important. Be transparent about your business's green practices by telling your customers exactly what you are doing and displaying the measurable impact.

Certification by third parties, through various agencies such as the Green Restaurant Association, Green Key Global, Leaders in Environmentally Accountable Foodservice (LEAF), and Leadership in Energy & Environmental Design (LEED), also lends credibility to your claims.

We will discuss traditional, emerging, and innovative marketing strategies in Chapter 12.

1.3 Staff retention

For many hospitality businesses that have made sustainability a key focus, the primary driver came from management who knew that value-based business operations would attract and retain workers. We have witnessed dramatic reversals in head-office thinking after focus groups listened to the younger staff express their views about a company's sustainability policy and behavior. Staff engagement is an important retention factor and green policies and practices have been shown to create positive engagement, because people feel better about working for businesses that have environmental values. Bold and innovative leadership engages staff to follow with confidence and to feel good about their place of employment, leading to better attitudes and enhanced retention.

1.4 Regulatory compliance

With a changing political and social landscape, environmental regulatory compliance is becoming a big factor for many businesses. Green initiatives such as recycling are mandatory in many jurisdictions. By taking a proactive approach, a restaurant, hotel, or resort can often avoid potential issues with regulators.

Although only some green practices are regulated today, issues such as water efficiency, energy conservation, recycled materials, and waste handling are key issues for utility companies as well as municipal and regional governments. For example, sorting paper from cardboard, and glass and plastic from other waste is required for restaurants on the southern tip of Vancouver Island and the Gulf Islands in British Columbia. Composting food waste is now a financial consideration for waste-removal contracts. With drought conditions occurring with greater frequency, water efficiency and even water rationing is a reality not only in parts of the southern US where it perhaps could be expected, but also in Washington State and British Columbia. Continued energy shortages and brownouts have implications of increased regulation for energy use by businesses.

1.5 Grants

Linked to regulatory compliance, governments and utility companies offer different levels of incentives and grants, varying from place to place and year to year. The commonality about grants is that early adopters are generally the major beneficiaries. Once behavior becomes normal, then habits become rules, and the grants that were used to incentivize changes in behavior will no longer be required or available.

1.6 Financial benefits

The financial benefits of going green are a powerful incentive. However, going green should be considered a process and we encourage you to start with the easy steps that will have the highest and fastest returns, often referred to as the "low hanging fruit." If those savings are then invested in larger and more costly initiatives with a higher but longer-term return on investment (ROI), the greening can be self-financed until the point that your goals are reached and you have a green business with improved efficiency, better staff retention, a loyal customer base, and improved profits.

To make your dollar go further, you can install green systems and materials that reduce energy consumption, which will reduce your energy bills. New efficient systems also increase your profits and the value of your assets.

1.7 More reasons to go green

Here are some additional reasons to go green now:

- It is easier than you think: It has never been easier to go green than it is today; qualified help is readily available and there are ever increasing options.

- To be competitive: A green business is rewarding; ask anyone who has improved the sustainability of their business and he or she will tell you that people respond well to green businesses.

- The health benefits: Going green is good for your own health, for your staff, and for your customers.

- Timing: Going green now will give you a competitive advantage because tomorrow may be too late for your business to adapt.

- Do the right thing: Those who see the planet and commerce as an interdependent system know that going green today is the right thing to do.

The following chapters will help you improve your hospitality business and the planet by going green.

People, Planet, Prosperity

 The payback model which dominates the green movement is the triple-bottom-line — people, planet, prosperity. As you will see, the paybacks to greening your business are threefold and they can be a game-changer in today's economy. Success for many business owners is not just about making money. Measuring the three Ps can give you perspective on the health and vitality of your business and the impact it has on the world.

The triple-bottom-line perspective has redefined success as more than strictly capitalistic. It implies that business can not only make money, but also have a positive impact on society and the planet. If we measure planet and society factors as we measure and count our money, we start to treat them with equal importance.

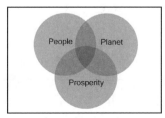

Figure 1: People, Planet, Prosperity

1. People

People are the lifeline of hospitality. Your staff and suppliers are as critical as your customers. If you map all of the connections that a single hospitality company has within a community, you will see a dense web of interconnections and relationships with other hospitality businesses, government and tourism agencies, local business groups, schools, transportation companies, linen companies, food suppliers, landscapers, and the list goes on.

A hospitality company has incredible potential to make a positive impact because it is at the nexus of a community. It forms a hub of people, and those people rely on your business in one way or another. Your social values and how your business interacts with people can make a big difference. Your business has the ability to impact the lives of hundreds of people. Consider your social values:

- What impression do you want to have on people?
- What do you want to leave in the wake of your business?
- What will be different in your community because your business exists?
- What issues can you help solve?
- How will your employees feel about their own lives after working for your company?

Case Study

Inn at Laurel Point, Victoria, British Columbia

The Inn at Laurel Point created a unique program called the "Courage Rate" for cancer patients who visit the city for treatment. People from nearby towns have to travel into the city for cancer treatments and stay overnight, but hotel rooms are often not covered by health care insurance. The Inn at Laurel Point felt these people, who are battling cancer, should have a comfortable place to rest after treatment so it introduced the Courage Rate to make their stays affordable. The Inn also offers complementary stays for patients who are struggling to make ends meet. Courage Rate customers have called Inn at Laurel Point staff "extended family" after such a heartwarming experience in a time when they needed support the most.

Hospitality businesses can consider the following initiatives for these groups to have a positive impact on society:

Employees:

- Introduce opportunities for staff training and career advancement.
- Allow employees to volunteer for one to three days per year on company time, for charities of their choice.
- Additional health benefits for committed employees.
- Provide free fruit and healthy food in the staff room.
- Install bike racks and provide transit passes for employees.
- Become a family-friendly workplace. Consider daycare allocations, or make it accessible and affordable for employees who are new parents. Introduce a progressive maternity/paternity policy.
- Survey staff every year to solicit feedback on how the workplace can be improved to reduce stress and maintain a positive work environment. Implement the changes you can to your workplace.

Customers:

- Include one meal on your menu that is healthy and affordable for anyone.
- Inform customers of what they can do to volunteer or take part in the community through supporting green companies, reducing waste, and/or volunteering for a cause.

Suppliers:

- Purchase from ethical vendors that have strong environmental and social practices.
- Support small-scale vendors and farmers in your community.
- Create a standard policy that requires all vendors to follow laws of human and environmental rights.

Community:

- Host an annual event to raise funds for a cause that is important to your local community.
- Create a special menu item or room package that donates profits to a local cause; allow employees to vote or choose the cause.
- Promote sustainable development in discussions with local government officials and business associations.

Businesses that have gone green have experienced increased staff retention and higher overall productivity. Integrating values into how the workplace operates allows employees to engage in a purpose beyond the duties of the job. The top employees today want more than a salary; they want purpose.

When you consider training costs, severance payments, job-search posting fees, and management time for interviews, staff retention benefits can greatly lower costs. In turn, that money can go towards increased raises, benefits, and other people-related costs. A loyal and engaged workforce also shines through in customer service. The whole atmosphere is affected with a more positive and lively energy.

Many studies have indicated that workers, especially millennials, exhibit a different set of professional values. They are more motivated by personal values, ethics, and purpose beyond the paycheck. They see a job as a place to exercise their values and unleash their passions. Heightened awareness and environmental education means that young employees respect companies with credible and visible sustainable strategies.

As the tourism industry continues to expand, it is important for every business to foster a culture of social well-being and sustainability. I visited an array of ethical hospitality businesses across North and Central America that valued employees like extended family. They had greater customer loyalty; the employees were more supportive of one another; employees took initiative and generated new ideas for the companies in their spare time; and overall, the businesses were a more pleasant place to work.

2. Planet

From the poles to the tropics, the impacts of climate change are evident and expanding. These changes create an imbalance in the earth's natural cycles and affect the entire planet. Even without the notion of climate change in mind, the pressure on natural resources has an impact on the hospitality business. Rising food costs, higher utility bills due to energy and water shortages, and rising insurance premiums are just a few ways these changes will result in business challenges.

Being a green business and protecting the planet is also about industry resilience. Ultimately, working to localize the food chain, reduce energy and water costs, become more self-sufficient with off-grid energy sources, and create more natural spaces for guests to enjoy will all result in a stronger business.

Due to climate change and concerns around pollution, much of the focus of the green movement has been directed toward lowering carbon-based energy and resource usage, managing waste and water, and improving air quality. As carbon-based energy and other resources continue to fluctuate unpredictably, lowering use by reducing demand and improving conservation efficiency is both economically and ecologically prudent. Our planet, more than ever, needs all of us to pitch in and take care of our own little corner. Even the most bottom-line driven and hard-nosed businessperson today must come to terms with these new pressures on commerce and recognize that finite and diminishing resources require a conservation plan built into the way a business operates. This planet is our home, so let's ensure that our hospitality businesses practice good housekeeping.

There is an ever-growing list of sustainable behavioral and methodological changes as well as improved technologies and equipment which can have results that range from minor to dramatic. A simple and very low-cost example are hands free, low-flow vanity faucets in public restrooms; they significantly reduce water use. The taps turn themselves on and off and get all the energy they need to operate simply from the lights in the bathrooms. With a higher investment, a business can install a solar hot water or photovoltaic system. To power a significant portion of energy requirements in a hotel or restaurant, an up-front investment is needed, but this can have a great long-term return on investment and will reduce the carbon footprint of the building. Consider the planet's bottom line for your business as you explore the following chapters, which discuss solutions in greater detail.

3. Prosperity

Of all the topics we will discuss from a green perspective, prosperity should really need no explanation to anyone in business although this important topic was often overlooked in the early days of the green movement. The story used to go like this: Going green is a novelty that costs too much money and compromises the financial bottom line. Today, that is simply not true because a strong case can be made for green investments, most notably in the area of lower operating cost.

When I began promoting green hospitality, although there were measurable cost savings to be had, the initial investment was substantial and presented serious obstacles to client uptake. Many alternative products and technologies were only available from Germany or Vermont. Today the only real impediment to green investment is inertia and habitual behavior.

The Dictionary of Sustainability Management[1] defines payback period as the following:

"An accounting term indicating the time required to recoup an investment. It is expressed as a ratio of investment cost to savings or income (usually annually). For example, if a new high-efficiency boiler costs $10,000 to install and saves $2,500 per year in fuel, the payback period is four years. Payback periods are critical to environmental and energy efficiency. Currently, conventions of short-term business thinking look at time periods less than common payback periods for alternative energy and other sustainability improvements. Until businesspeople consider longer term periods of time or new technologies to reduce the payback period of 'green' technologies, there will continue to be lackluster interest in many sustainable solutions."

3.1 Long-term sustainability

Change can involve significant costs so the primary question for any business is: Is this cost worth the investment of time and money? For example, new LED lightbulbs are more expensive than standard incandescent and fluorescent bulbs; however, LEDs use far less energy to create the same amount of light so the investment in LED lights has a short payback period because of the energy savings. This cost is sometimes mitigated by grants from utilities looking to lower commercial energy use. There are also labor efficiencies because LED lightbulbs last far longer which lowers maintenance costs.

Our model suggests a planned and staged investment in these costs whereby savings from the first steps are used to finance or at least justify subsequent steps.

For building owners looking at costs to increase efficiency, there are virtually no proven green initiatives that cannot have a life-cycle payback model that is shorter than a mortgage. Even some of the most costly steps such as geothermal energy, photovoltaic solar energy, commercial heat pumps, waste-energy recovery, and other infrastructure improvements are proving to be good investments for those businesses which have taken a leadership position and been among the first to make these big changes. For example, in Victoria, the Grand Pacific Hotel has installed solar panels on its roof, and added heat pumps in its maintenance room for massive summer energy savings. The hotel is already looking at a shorter payback period than originally expected.

---

1 "Payback Period," *The Dictionary of Sustainability Management*, accessed August 2015. www.sustainabilitydictionary.com/payback-period/

Table 2
Measuring Financial and Environmental Investment Options

Initiative (Example)	Cost (materials and installation)	Annual Utility/ Material Cost Saving	Annual Environmental Savings (water, energy, or carbon)	Total Payback Period
New boiler system	$25,000	$11,000 (natural gas)	450 GJ natural gas	2.3 years
Switch all kitchen lighting to LED	$3,000	$1,505 (electricity)	13,000 kWh	4 years
Change toilets to low-flow models	$7,500	$4,500 (water)	1.5 million liters	1.7 years

It's worth doing the math on investments with a higher price tag to determine your long-term return on investment, taking into account the life expectancy of the system. This can help you make sound financial decisions and prioritize the areas of operations you can shift to reduce environmental impact.

We use the term "prosperity" instead of "profit" because of its broader definition of "thriving" as a company. To prosper is to gain wealth in the many ways it presents itself such as natural capital, social capital, and financial capital. The three are interlinked and interdependent, and can work in sync to benefit your business and grow all three bottom lines. Your business can reduce costs, increase marketability, and create a culture of sustainability by taking steps to become a triple-bottom-line business. A more sustainable planet, social stability, and a more profitable business is a good recipe for long-term prosperity.

Table 3 shows you the metrics for measuring your business's triple-bottom-line success.

Table 3
Metrics for Measuring Triple-Bottom-Line Success

People	Planet	Prosperity
Employee satisfaction Overall employees' health (e.g., sick days) Employee retention rate	Total Carbon Footprint (tonnes of CO_2e) Total energy, water, and fuel use Ratio of recycled waste versus trash	Gross profit margin Year-over-year revenue growth Returning customers Annual utility bill savings

2
Climate Change

The success of tourism and hospitality businesses is highly dependent on climate. Nearly every type of business in the sector is more profitable with good, stable weather. Even a local coffee shop will see huge fluctuations in business between a sunny and a rainy day. Hospitality is a sector that relies on people leaving their homes to experience other places, and predictable weather makes those places desirable.

The volatility of climate change will have adverse effects on business and communities; however, the science has shown that we still have choices and if we act with urgency, we can reduce the harmful impacts of climate change on our communities, businesses, and natural environments.

We know that the last three decades have continued to warm the earth's surface and anthropogenic (human-caused) greenhouse gas emission sources have increased drastically since the pre-industrial era. With population growth and economic development, emissions have risen. The impacts of greenhouse gases such as carbon dioxide, nitrous oxide, and methane include ocean acidification and loss of coral reefs, the melting of permafrost and glaciers, and sea levels rising. With the current pressures on our natural systems to support human populations (e.g., fishing, logging, mineral extraction, agriculture) we cannot afford to jeopardize these natural resources. The loss of many species, including amphibians, fish, mammals, birds, and reptiles, have been attributed to the ripple effects of climate change, deforestation, over-harvesting, and pollution.

The Intergovernmental Panel on Climate Change (IPCC) is the world's thought leader on climate change and global climate modeling. Its "Climate Change 2014 *Synthesis Report* Fifth Assessment Report," shows different trajectories depending on how humanity as a whole decides to act on climate change. According to the report the "warming of the climate system is unequivocal, and since the 1950s, many of the observed changes are unprecedented over decades to millennia. The atmosphere and ocean have warmed, the amounts of snow and ice have diminished, and sea level has risen."[1] Government policy, industrial processes, consumer behavior, and business operations all play a role in determining the path we take. We can work towards a low-carbon economy, or we can continue with business as usual, and pay the price.

Table 4 shows the key sources of greenhouse gasses.

Table 4
Key Sources of Greenhouse Gasses

Greenhouse Gas	Key Sources
Carbon Dioxide (CO_2)	Fossil fuel combustion (e.g., transportation, heating), industrial processes, forestry.
Nitrous Oxide (N_2O)	Agriculture, industrial and chemical production (e.g., making of nylon and commercial fertilizers).
Methane (CH_4)	Raising livestock (e.g., cattle, buffalo, sheep, goats), landfill waste from homes and businesses, natural gas production and distribution, coal mining.
Fluorinated Gases (F-Gases)	Foaming agents, coolers, pesticides, and fire extinguishers.

Climate change amplifies the risks of events that can alter our everyday lives and the success of businesses. Inland flooding, water shortages, storm surges, extreme rain, landslides, and tsunamis — these events will become more frequent if we do not act now on climate

---

1 "Climate Change 2014 *Synthesis Report* Fifth Assessment Report," Intergovernmental Panel on Climate Change (IPCC), 2015, accessed September 2015. http://ar5-syr.ipcc.ch/topic_observedchanges.php

change and prepare our cities and businesses to be more resilient and self-sufficient.

We need to mitigate risk by lowering the carbon footprint of our communities, lifestyles, and businesses. Who better to lead this change than the hospitality sector? Because the businesses in this sector are inherently desirable destinations and gathering places, they have an incredible potential for inspiring changes in everyday human behavior and lifestyle choices. The industry can also impact government policy and influence sustainable development in local communities. The hospitality sector can spearhead change and lead us on a different trajectory as well as to a more sustainable future.

1. Hospitality and Climate Change

The hospitality industry often sets trends and establishes best practices. It depends on agriculture, farming, fishing, and hunting. It also involves cooling, shipping, processing, packaging, more shipping, storing, cooking, and wasting. Every step in the food-supply chain has a carbon footprint.

Samples 1, 2, and 3 show you examples of a carbon footprint of a hotel, restaurant, and tour operator.

Sample 1
Carbon Footprint of a Hotel

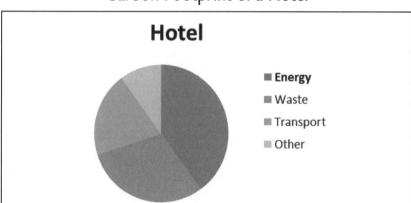

Sample 2
Carbon Footprint of a Restaurant

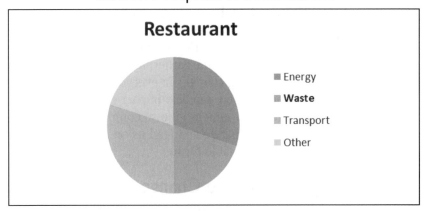

Sample 3
Carbon Footprint of a Tour Operator

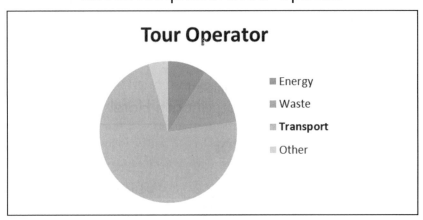

The carbon footprint profile of every business is different; although, there are clear themes in hotels, tours, and restaurants. A fast food restaurant will typically have a greater carbon footprint in the waste category compared to a full-service, sit-down restaurant. A hotel powered by fossil-fuel combustion will have a greater footprint than a hotel powered by hydroelectricity or geothermal energy.

Every business can assess its carbon footprint and find key areas in which to reduce emissions; areas such as waste, energy, transportation, refrigeration, travel, and paper consumption.

The following are some ways to lower your carbon footprint:

- Composting, recycling, and reducing waste.
- Using clean energy and energy-efficient appliances.
- Providing green options for staff commutes (cycling, transit, carpooling).
- Reducing and/or providing smaller portions of beef and lamb in restaurants (more on this in Section 2.).
- Using local and seasonal produce supplied within a 100-mile radius, which reduces use of food items that need to be transported by air.

2. The Carbon Footprint of Food

The shifts in weather patterns and creation of extreme conditions such as droughts, floods, heat waves, and cold spells are already straining global food production. Recent studies have linked climate change to a predicted decline in yields of crops such as wheat, maize, rice, and soy. In the last 50 years, our food chain has become long and disparate from what we used to know. The food we consume on a regular basis is grown on the other side of the planet, and travels long distances to reach our plates. This causes enormous amounts of greenhouse-gas emissions because of transport by ground, sea, and air.

We are already seeing the impacts of climate change on ocean acidification, which is destroying coral reefs — a critical breeding and feeding ground for many marine species. We are seeing pollinators such as bees at risk and, in turn, we are losing major fruit production. The weather patterns that shift greatly due to climate change are causing drought, and more agricultural land is becoming desert. These changes not only affect costs, they affect the future of our food-supply chain. We could run out of almonds, bananas, and other vulnerable staples to our diet if we don't start to address climate change and stabilize the food-supply chain.

The increased vulnerability of our food supply to the impacts of climate change adds more alarming dilemmas. Price fluctuations, shortages, and increased pesticide needs are only some repercussions we can expect. Every restaurant, hotel, clubhouse, resort, and gourmet food truck (with a few exceptions of farm-to-table sourcing) completely relies on the global food trade. Production of food worldwide is threatened more than ever by the global climate change. One soon realizes that the hospitality business will need to adapt and change.

So how does a hospitality company address the carbon footprint of the food it buys? How do you shift to a lower-carbon approach without compromising quality, price point, and accessibility?

Hospitality can affect the way people eat both on a local level and as part of the international food-supply chain. As you assess your sourcing and food suppliers, keep these things in mind:

- Beef, lamb, and dairy have high carbon footprints, which is why the carbon footprint of vegan and vegetarian diets can be half of that of a meat-eating diet.

- Even produce can be grown with massive energy inputs. A hothouse tomato can have a five times higher carbon footprint than a tomato grown in season.

- Virtually every step in processing food has a carbon footprint due to energy input; transportation; and chilling, cooking, and packaging.

- Food grown closer to source will have a smaller embedded carbon footprint.

- Choosing food-service providers with low-emission vehicles, and providers that already service your area, will reduce additional emissions from servicing your business.

3. What Can You Do?

Some of the top restaurants and hotels in the world are confronting the topic of climate change and food security by incorporating green business practices and strengthening their relationships with local suppliers. Those leaders are not yet in the majority, but they represent a new imperative and a great example for the sector.

Summary of what your business can do:

- Assess your contribution to climate change by measuring your carbon footprint.

- Make a plan to reduce your carbon footprint over the next 6 to 12 months.

- Review your supply chain. Where does your supply originate? Can you find and nurture more sustainable options?

- Support local food production and strengthen your local food infrastructure. Many people are looking for regional experiences, so use local craft brewers and winemakers.

- Review your waste management. Find ways to reduce waste and recycle wherever possible.
- Conserve energy and fuel in all areas of your operation.
- Reduce transportation in the supply chain, staff commuting, and corporate travel.
- Review your lighting, heating, cooling, kitchen equipment, and everything that contributes to your energy use and replace these with more efficient equipment whenever you need to repair parts or upgrade equipment, or whenever you can afford to invest in energy savings.
- Measure the changes to your company's carbon footprint over time.
- Enjoy the feeling that comes from becoming a green business!

Success in the hospitality sector, in both the short and long term, depends on serious efforts to shift business practices and take action to mitigate the impacts of climate change. Your business can join the ranks of great companies that have boldly embedded action into their day-to-day operations.

Those who plan for and adapt to change are the most likely survivors in any form of evolution. The following chapters will help your business make a positive difference and set an example for other businesses to follow.

3
How the Hospitality Industry Can Change the World

My last trip to Costa Rica changed the way I view hospitality. It was there that I realized that of all of the sectors I work with, hospitality has the greatest ability to change the world today. The operations of a single restaurant, hotel, or tour can seem inconsequential to the world at large, but the opposite is true.

Every hospitality business is a place where people congregate. It is their first entry to a place and it influences how they experience, view, and act within it. For example, a hotel that fosters active transportation by having bicycles available for rent changes how guests will experience the place they are visiting.

The infrastructure of hospitality such as major resorts, restaurants in a downtown community, food-service facilities, and docks for marine tours largely dictate how entire communities and cities develop. Hospitality businesses are at the core of communities, at major ports, and destinations on the fringes of society. They influence how we develop and grow our communities. Power sources, transportation routes, residential neighborhoods, and community planning are all important to the whereabouts of hospitality.

In Costa Rica, I saw how hospitality can not only change lives, but entire cities and the local environment. For instance, Latitude 10 Resort is a small, high-end resort in Santa Teresa. Even though that sounds similar to other small resorts, Latitude 10 has a different perspective. It is part of the Cayuga Collection in Latin America. This group of accommodations understands and values the impact it has on the world. They hire locals and help them grow into managerial roles. Every resort is operated with environmental principles — they have locally made natural toiletries and soap products, and they are energy-efficient and use rain barrels to capture water. Some locations compost food scraps from the kitchens for use in the soil in their gardens, which are lush with native plants to provide a home for local species. Everything is carefully designed with the environment in mind, and it changes the guest experience. Through the recommendations of the hotel, guests see Costa Rica differently such as experiencing the wildlife that visits the hotel, taking eco-tours, and having opportunities to volunteer in the community. The guests staying there actually make a positive difference in Costa Rica; instead of just taking resources and exploiting local populations, the resort is designed to give back.

Hospitality, as a global industry, can share best practices and set the stage for hundreds of other businesses. This is a highly connected industry, and a highly competitive one. Although there are millions of businesses worldwide, one business can change how many others operate. For example, if one hotel in a community can prove that solar thermal technology is viable from a logistics and cost perspective, dozens of others may do the same. Hospitality businesses typically have many vendors that regularly supply them such as linen providers, cleaning services, food delivery, electricians, plumbers, landscapers, bakers, wedding planners, and dozens more. A policy to purchase from sustainable vendors can affect action throughout the supply chain servicing the hotel.

Hospitality is a gateway for customers to experience the world, for employees to grow careers, and for cities to develop sustainably. Every hospitality business is highly connected to other businesses — through peer businesses and an extensive supply chain. The ripple effects of environmental and socially responsible practices in a hotel, restaurant, or tour radiates far and wide. That is why hospitality is poised to change the world.

The environmental movement in hospitality is part of a broader seismic shift in the industry today. Hotels used to primarily offer the "home away from home" experience — comforts similar to home. Now, hotels are more experiential; they offer unique experiences to visitors. Hotels no longer offer just the commodity bed, below-par continental breakfast, and parking space. Hotels and restaurants today are a gateway to experience a place. They offer communal spaces to socialize and features that spark our curiosity and feed our intellect: books, unique magazines, infographic displays, music, art, cooking classes, exercise classes, and healthy lifestyle practices. A new breed of hotels and restaurants are changing what it means to host guests with outstanding cuisine, high-tech features, green practices, and superb design.

1. Green Leaders in the Hospitality Industry

The hospitality industry with its hotels, resorts, restaurants, club-houses, spas, pubs, and lounges, combined with art galleries (our modern temples of culture), are changing the world of architecture. Wherever you live and work, the most likely candidate for trendsetting architectural design style in your community is likely to be a gallery, restaurant, or hotel. A combination of factors, not the least of which is competition, lead the hospitality industry toward constant reinvention and innovation. These changes are now starting to take sustainability and the green movement seriously.

Case Study: Las Vegas

When MGM announced its largest investment in Las Vegas called CityCenter it was a surprise to the gaming and hotel industry that the project would be Leadership in Energy & Environmental Design (LEED) registered. At the Green Hospitality Conference and Tradeshow, MGM's vice president told attendees that the decision was not based on idealism, it was economics that drove the decision to build a sustainable, green development on a massive scale.

Their leadership had the foresight to make this move more than a decade ago, before the water crisis which is now gripping the Colorado basin. The MGM project was built with water-efficient plumbing fixtures, but its resorts encompass much more than water efficiency.

MGM's statement:

"MGM Resorts International is committed to being a leader in environmental stewardship, bringing value to our shareholders and the communities in which we operate. Created to increase the sustainability of our company, Green Advantage is MGM Resorts environmental responsibility platform that focuses on reducing our consumption of the planet's limited resources through innovation, education and efficiency. Green Advantage ensures that we incorporate environmentally responsible practices that effectively lower our carbon footprint throughout all of operations. We believe that a greener business is a better business."

"To achieve our sustainability goals, we have focused our efforts on five core areas that contribute to our footprint. These five core areas drive our continuous improvements and the result is that hundreds of best practices have been implemented and MGM Resorts properties have reduced annual emissions of CO_2E by more than 100,000 metric tons."[1]

MGM has received six LEED Gold certifications amongst many other sustainability awards and recognitions:

"CityCenter Las Vegas earned the prestigious Leadership in Energy and Environmental Design — New Construction (LEED-NC) Gold certification rating for six buildings within the CityCenter campus, including the ARIA hotel tower and convention center. LEED certification is awarded by the US Green Building Council based on a project's environmental design, construction and operations. Today, CityCenter is the largest LEED-NC Gold certified new construction project in the world and is truly a ground-breaking achievement in the gaming and hospitality industry. By designing and building ARIA and the CityCenter campus to the stringent environmental design and construction criteria of LEED Gold, MGM Resorts International has set the standard for environmentally responsible growth and for large-scale development efforts around the world."[2]

These case srudies show not just that hospitality can lead change, but that indeed the hospitality industry is pulling its weight in changing the world. When people visit Las Vegas, they get ideas about the future of construction.

---

1 "Green Meetings & Sustainability," MGM Grand Hotel and Casino, accessed August 2015. http://ddtest.mgmgrand.com/meetings/green-key.aspx
2 "Sustainability Awards and Recognition," MGM Resorts International, accessed October, 2015. htth://mgmresorts.com/company/awards-recognitions.htm

Utility companies and governments reward this leadership with incentive and grant programs that favor first adopters of new, sustainable technologies and practices. For example, in Toronto, Canada, incentives have been made available from Toronto Hydro and Toronto Water to the hospitality business. Those who took advantage of these incentives enhanced their return on investment and reduced the payback time for retrofits. In addition, they benefited as they became a case study, receiving earned media coverage and marketing.

Perhaps better known throughout the hospitality industry is Green Key Global. This organization assists hotels with environmental initiatives and marketing efforts. The Green Key Eco-Rating Program and Green Key Meetings Program are graduated rating systems designed to recognize green hotels, motels, and resorts that are committed to improving their environmental performance. Green Key Global is one of many certification organizations that can rate your efforts and offer the benefits of certified recognition for your hotel or resort.

Certification is one way that change is recognized and multiplied because it raises the bar across the sector and creates a new baseline for green business practices. For example, TripAdvisor has a program called GreenLeaders which showcases a variety of eco-friendly hotels and bed and breakfasts, from budget to luxury; all are committed to green practices such as recycling, providing local and organic food, and installing electric vehicle charging stations.

In California, Bar Agricole has taken a leadership role in the South of Market district of San Francisco with their vertical food integration from farm to table. Each spring, Bar Agricole pays selected local farmers for one year's worth of produce, meat, and poultry.

The integration of local food sourcing within trendsetting restaurants owned and operated by market leaders is not just changing the communities where they operate; they are also inspiring international clientele who travel from other cities to patronize the best restaurants in San Francisco.

Also deserving of recognition is the San Francisco restaurant Chez Panisse and its founder and chef, Alice Waters, as an original leader and advocate for a food economy that is "good, clean, and fair."[3] Waters supports local ranchers and farmers who are dedicated to sustainable agriculture.

Another leadership example worth noting is the former General Manager of the Fairmont Empress Hotel, Martin LeClerc. He implemented

---

3 Alice Waters, Executive Chef, Founder and Owner, Chez Panisse, accessed August 2015. http://www.chezpanisse.com/about/alice-waters/

two model programs that are now catching on with other hotels. The first was an artist-in-residence program. The second leadership action LeClerc initiated was more significant to the green movement; this was the introduction of honey bees and hives on the lawn of the hotel. The hotel placed working hives in the center of the busiest tourist district of Victoria, the Inner Harbour. The hives were installed with "viewing rooms" for visitors to look at a cross-section of the hive in action. Several beehives generate hundreds of pounds of honey for the hotel's restaurant and famous afternoon tea. LeClerc explained that he could have easily sourced and purchased local and organic honey, but this intentional green initiative was started by the hotel because the hives in the city center would help raise awareness about pollination and the important roles bees play in our ecology. Victoria is famous for its spring blossoms, but without the bees, there would be no pollination for those blossoms.

1.1 Eco-luxury tourism

Eco-luxury tourism is becoming more popular with ethical travelers who want to stay in places that are ecologically and socially responsible. This type of travel has opened many doors in the greening of the hospitality market, because at the luxury end of the market people expect to pay more as long as the experience is worthwhile. For example, at the Clayoquot Wilderness Resort you don't get a room, you get a tent! This resort is committed to restoring the land and all areas of the resort operations are low-impact on the environment. From high-efficiency furnaces to toilets that compost waste materials, this resort's goals are conservancy-driven. The company, Ecolux Hotels, is an independent organization that assesses the world's greenest luxury hotels and provides consumers with information on which hotels are genuinely eco-friendly and which ones are greenwashing.

2. Can Your Business Help to Change the World?

Your business doesn't need to be as large as MGM or as visionary as Alice Waters or Martin LeClerc, to do its part and contribute to a better world. Every little step helps, whether you are a dishwasher who remembers to turn off the tap or a chef who shifts to a seasonal menu. You may own a hotel chain and set a bold green policy statement for your brand to follow.

Recognize the challenge of climate change to the hospitality industry, and do what you can to conserve resources and continually update your practices. These changes can enhance your offering to your patrons, and position your business as a progressive company that inspires other businesses to raise the bar.

4
Greening Your Building

The design of green buildings has evolved significantly in the last three decades. According to the US Green Building Council (USGBC), buildings consume 13.6 percent of drinkable water, 40 percent of the raw materials, and 41 percent of the energy consumed.[1] The primary reasons that green buildings are increasing in popularity are a combination of lower operating costs, improved building performance, and the marketability of green buildings. The cost premium of building a green building has dropped dramatically compared to the first hyper-green buildings a few decades ago. As utility costs continue to rise, the benefits of owning or leasing a smart green building in terms of cost savings and energy efficiency also increase. With predicted energy and climate challenges ahead, environmental and efficient building design will make your company more resilient and prepared for the future. A greener building is an intelligent long-term development strategy to hedge against potential weather events and the rise in energy costs.

Advances in solar-energy, geothermal, heat pumps, and improved energy efficiencies represent the largest potential savings to the hospitality sector, an industry that as a whole is very energy intensive. Start

1 "Green Building Facts," US Green Building Council (USGBC), accessed August 2015. www.usgbc.org/articles/green-building-facts

by understanding how your business operates and look for opportunities to enhance performance, first with conservation, then with alternative low-carbon energy production. Over time, your building will become more resilient and energy efficient.

The suggestions in this chapter refer to both new construction and renovation options. Whether you lease a small commercial space, or plan to develop a large plot of land, there will be options to improve how your hospitality venture operates.

1. Site Selection

Site selection, urban planning, building design, and orientation strongly impact the performance of your hospitality business over its lifetime. Careful consideration to aspects of sustainable design will identify opportunities to use natural features, and construct with the land, rather than against it. Look for natural features such as creeks and trees that can be retained and used in the design. There are many considerations that go into project design and the environmental aspect of every project is greatly affected by many small decisions at the start of the project.

The following are some things to consider when searching for a site:

- Proximity to transportation hubs and connections.
- Availability of natural light and sun exposure.
- Proximity to a water source; they can be utilized for passive hydrothermal heating and cooling.
- Natural surroundings and ecology. How can your development improve the natural surroundings rather than simply exploit them?
- Local government urban-development plans and how your development will fit within them. Can you advance sustainability objectives in collaboration with your local government?
- What utilities or power sources are accessible or present at the current site? Are sustainable sources such as wind, geothermal, or microhydro an option?

When designing a project, it is important to decide, at the beginning, what type of community and space you are trying to create. Will your final product foster connections and support an active lifestyle? Will it promote health and well-being? Will it be integrated with the local ecology and support synergies between the natural world and business? These are all critical questions that will influence the outcome of your project. Prepare these objectives first and then design your project to meet those objectives.

An important consideration for hospitality businesses is the facade. New construction in hospitality is shifting away from the car-centric model with narrow sidewalks, wide streets, and vast parking lots. It is shifting toward a model that is a more human-centric design with plants, borders, patios, common spaces, vast gardens, walking pathways, bicycle routes; and many areas for people to congregate, interact, and explore the building and outside environment. This human-centric rather than car-centric design can benefit your business by harnessing one of the best market forces in hospitality today: People attracting other people. As was discussed in Chapter 3, hospitality today is more than a commodity, it is an experience.

2. Construction

The teardown of past structures and the process of building new ones can be hugely wasteful and energy intensive. Even if the end result is a green building, the construction process can damage nearby ecosystems and have a massive carbon footprint.

In all new construction projects, small or large, consider the following practices:

- Control run-off with Silt Socks, which block and filter debris from polluting stormwater drains, rivers, lakes, and other waterways.
- Salvage existing materials such as wood, metals, concrete, glass, and stone for reuse in your current construction.
- Hire contractors with credentials and solid environmental practices and policies. Include these criteria and question what they will do as part of your bid tender.
- Most construction sites have one, giant, catch-all waste bin that goes to the landfill. Recycle on-site with bins for all streams of waste that will be developed on-site (e.g., wood, drywall, wire). Give all trade crews information about what materials can go into each bin. Let them know they will need to sort the materials if they don't comply.
- Energy supply on-site: Consider using biodiesel generators or other low-impact energy sources on-site, rather than burning fossil fuels.

3. Building Performance and Design

Your building will have many functions — heating, cooling, charging, venting, pumping, and draining. These functions of moving materials and energy throughout a space all have an impact. Think of your building as a living, breathing system. Looking at the flow of materials, energy, waste, and water, people can help visualize opportunities to optimize performance. For example, consider the flow of air through your building. Doors are opened, air is heated in one area, cooled in another, and vented in various areas. Looking at the air flow as a system, you may find air is being heated in some areas just to be expelled by nearby doors or vents. This immediately expelled air is consuming energy and not effectively improving your indoor environment.

Similarly, you can look at your water flow. Water falls onto the roof and runs down the drains to the outdoor environment. Where does it go? Could that wasted water be intercepted and used for another purpose? Working to "close the loop" on your air flows and capture what is wasted can improve your building performance and reduce energy use without heavy investment.

3.1 Energy production

Most of us do not put much thought into where our energy comes from. Ironically, the connected grid system that powers our communities disconnects us from where and how the energy is actually produced. In every grid system, there is a level of uncertainty. What impact does the energy you use have on the world? Is it a sustainable source of energy for the future? What natural systems does your energy use displace? Will the cost continue to rise?

Energy invariably comes up in conversations about climate change because most conventional energy sources are major greenhouse gas emitters. Fossil fuel-based energy production by combustion of oil, natural gas, and coal is still widespread in Europe, North America, Asia, and other regions. If your local area is powered by one of these sources, conserving energy and supplementing your power source with renewable energy will immediately lower the carbon footprint of your business.

There is a spectrum of carbon intensities from different energy sources. On the carbon-intensive end of the spectrum are coal, oil, and gas; on the lower end you find hydro, nuclear, wind, solar photovoltaic, solar thermal, and geothermal.

Renewable energy is important because of the benefits it provides to the environment, to the local economy, and to energy security. Renewable energy will not run out as the sun and wind will always exist. Fossil fuel sources of energy are finite and will someday be depleted. There is also a strong community investment aspect to green energy.

Local renewable energy investments are spent on materials and local workmanship to build and maintain technologies, rather than on costly energy imports. This means your energy dollars stay local and help create jobs and increase local economic prosperity. In countries such as Germany, development projects support and purchase renewable energy technologies from local companies. Germany has a strong export market for renewable technology products and services, which is helping build a green economy, and create green jobs for the future.

Renewable energy technologies such as solar and heat-exchange systems have continually evolved over the last 30 years. Countries such as Denmark have made major strides to increase the amount of renewable energy supply to local communities, and many projects are community owned.

The viability and effectiveness of most renewable energy technologies is dependent on geography and natural energy sources on-site. For example, solar energy availability is limited by your latitude location, sun orientation, and exposure. Other key factors include maintenance requirements of the systems and a range of installation costs. It is important to assess which systems are viable within your building, and which will generate the most power for the lowest cost, giving your business the best return on investment.

Take a look at Table 5. The return on investment for this example is: $112,500 (energy savings) - $32,500 (installation cost + annual maintenance) = $80,000 over 25 years.

Table 5
Assessing Alternative Energy Projects

Option	Installation Cost	Energy Generation	Total Energy Savings	Payback Time (years)	Maintenance Costs	Life Expectancy
Example: Solar PV	$25,000	5 kWh/day	$4,500/year ($112,500)	5.5 years	$300/year (7,500)	25 years

3.2 Photovoltaic solar panels

Photovoltaic (PV) solar panels generate electricity by the absorption of sunlight through silicone cells which are transferred to an electrical grid or a bank of batteries. The Hotel Grand Pacific in Victoria, British Columbia, recently installed a combination of solar panels on its roof and new heat pumps in its mechanical room. The solar panels generate energy and the heat pumps increase energy efficiency.

The pros of PV solar panels include the following:

- Passive energy gains requiring minimal cost inputs once installed.
- Resilient and relatively consistent supply of energy independent of grid system. For remote hotels and restaurants with inconsistent energy supply, solar is one of the best options.
- Low operating and low maintenance costs compared to other renewable energy systems.
- In basic systems, there are no mechanical moving parts, meaning limited breakdowns.
- Systems typically last 25 to 30 years.
- A solar installation is a green statement to staff and guests.

As you will see, there are fewer cons than pros to installing PV solar panels:

- Variability in energy gains dependent on the weather and amount of sunlight the system absorbs.
- High capital cost per kilowatt hour of electricity supply.

The cost of solar panels has previously been a significant barrier; however, the price has significantly dropped due to expanding markets in the US, Canada, and Europe and to less expensive production in China. A noticeable drop has occurred over the last five years, making the payback much more desirable for most North Americans. In 1977 the silicon PV cells in dollar-per-watt was $76.67; in 2013, it was $0.74.[2]

Germany's commitment to solar energy has been astounding, and has set the bar high for other countries. On some days, an impressive percentage of Germany's energy demand is being met by solar PV plants installed throughout the country.[3] Keep in mind, if you are concerned about a lack of sun in your area, most of North America has the same as or better levels of solar availability than Germany, so if it can work there, it can work here!

Look to a local solar contractor to assess your site and determine if you have a viable location for solar PV, the total installation cost, residual costs for repair and maintenance, and potential energy generation.

---

2 "13 Cost of Solar Panels & Cost of Solar Power Charts & Graphs," Zachary Shahan, Clean Technica, accessed October 2015. http://cleantechnica.com/2014/09/04/solar-panel-cost-trends-10-charts/
3 "Performance of Photovoltaics (PV) in Germany," SMA Solar Technology AG, accessed October 2015. www.sma.de/en/company/pv-electricity-produced-in-germany.html

Innovation: Solar Cooking

An old technology that has resurfaced recently is the solar oven. It works on the basic principle of sunlight providing the heat energy to cook or dry food. Essentially, the sun's energy is the fuel — a carbon-neutral alternative to combusting natural gas or wood. Solar cookers use reflective surfaces to direct the sun's energy towards the cooking chamber. Solar ovens can heat up to normal baking temperatures of 350 to 450 degrees. Personal/family size solar cookers are available on the market today, and more commercial models are being developed.

3.3 Solar hot water systems

Solar hot water (SHW) heats water or glycol. The heated liquid is then transferred from the solar panel to a hot water tank or to radiant floor heating. Using solar thermal as a passive, carbon-neutral heat source for water or in-floor heating can reduce the carbon footprint of your business if your conventional heat source is a fossil fuel.

If your business has high energy costs, solar thermal is a great investment and it can have a quick payback time.

The pros include the following:

- Can produce a strong return on investment.
- Carbon neutral energy source from the sun's heat.
- Generally long lasting with low-maintenance costs.

The cons include the following:

- System effectiveness can vary greatly. It is important to conduct a review of the different panel systems available and find one of high quality.
- These systems do require some maintenance. Systems that heat glycol must be tested regularly as the chemical can break down over time, and "burned" glycol can damage a system.

Simple solar thermal systems, common in Latin America and remote, off-grid communities, involve coils or rows of black piping filled with water that naturally heats with solar gains. These inexpensive systems are completely passive and ideal for heating pools or hot tubs.

3.4 Geo-exchange systems

Geothermal heat-exchange systems operate similar to refrigerators. Heat is drawn from inside your refrigerator and dispersed from the coils at the back. This is the same technology that is used in geo-exchange heating. The unique part of this technology is that the process can be reversed back and forth to provide heating and cooling. These systems take advantage of the ground's heating and cooling properties to heat or cool buildings. The "exchange" between the ground and the building is achieved by using a pump and compressor to move liquid and expel heat in the ground of the building.

Installing these systems can be expensive, as they either require drilling deep wells, or coiled loops installed horizontally over a wide area. The excavation required makes this an expensive technology to install in a retrofit project, which is why they are more common in new builds when site excavation is already occurring.

The pros include the following:

- Can produce a strong return on investment over the long term.
- Attractive "free energy" feature during resale of the building.
- Low environmental impact energy source.
- Generally long lasting.

There is only one con and that is the high capital cost to install the system.

You can learn more about geo-exchange systems online:

- Geoexchange (United States): www.geoexchange.org
- Canadian GeoExchange Coalition: www.geo-exchange.ca

3.5 Biomass or bioenergy

Another type of heating is biomass generation, which is the burning of organic materials to generate heat. In new biomass systems, combustion systems have been developed to minimize emissions and airborne particulate, resulting in a lower carbon footprint than early technologies.

Biomass boilers are relatively simple; the fuel enters the system (blown in or auger-fed) into a combustion chamber and is burnt at a high temperature. The ash is composted and the thermal energy is used to heat water, air, or oil for radiators.

Biomass systems can be appropriate where organic matter is produced on a regular basis. Hospitality businesses that include or are adjacent to agriculture, large greenhouses, wood and pulp mills, or that produce a large amount of organic waste themselves, may consider biomass a viable energy source. A number of different fuels can be burnt with the biomass boilers, such as wood waste, tree pruning, horse manure, wood pellets, agriculture waste, and other organic matter. For hotels and restaurants with high heating demands and the right organic material source, biomass is a good option.

3.6 Wind power

In 2014, the Hilton Fort Lauderdale Beach Resort raised six wind turbines on the rooftop of the 25-story hotel.[4] The Florida hotel stated that it expected the 52-foot tall turbines to power 5 to 10 percent of the energy needs of the hotel, or all of the building's lighting. Over time, turbines like this, in the right application, will reduce energy consumption and generate a return on investment.

In Seattle, Northwest Wind & Solar installed two rooftop turbines on the Hyatt Olive 8 hotel. In this arrangement, the exhaust air from the restaurant on the ground floor is vented out of the roof of the hotel and directed at the wind turbine, providing a continual gust that spins the blades. The unique spherical design of these turbines makes the blades appear solid as they rotate, which helps bats and birds evade the blades.

Wind-power generators need strong and consistent airstreams so most residential areas are not ideal because of trees, buildings, and other geographical features. A wind turbine will produce more power the higher it is and the faster the average wind speed is in the area. For example, an average speed of 8 mph may produce 550 kWh monthly whereas wind speeds at 14 mph could produce 2,280 kWh. Rooftops in areas with high average wind speeds, or a steady source of air from vents, can be ideal installation sites for wind power.

3.7 Indoor water and nature features

By adding a touch of nature and natural light indoors, you can create a tranquil environment and reduce workplace stress. What naturalists, romantics, and ecologists have been saying about the healing power of nature for centuries is now being scientifically proven as biologically and psychologically beneficial: Nature has healing powers. For example, during winter, many people enjoy sitting in sunrooms, solariums, atriums, and greenhouses.

---

4 "Wind Turbines Now Spinning at Hilton Hotel," Arlene Satchell, Sun Sentinel, accessed October 2015. http://articles.sun-sentinel.com/2014-01-31/business/fl-hilton-lauderdale-wind-turbines-opening-20140131_1_wind-turbines-hilton-worldwide-green-lodging-news

Water in an atrium space, combined with operating skylights or vents at the top of a space is the oldest and most natural form of air conditioning, based on the Roman atrium house model. The Parkside Hotel & Spa in Victoria, British Columbia, is a LEED-certified property and a TripAdvisor GreenLeaders Gold awarded facility because it uses a natural cooling effect in its wonderful atrium lobby (www.parkside victoria.com).

You can also add vegetation inside your establishment. Plants make oxygen from carbon dioxide, which is important for indoor air quality. They also remove pollutants from the air making them natural air filters of the highest order. Therefore, we recommend you review your landscaping opportunities inside your facility and consider plants and trees with low water needs that are appropriate to your bioregion and climate.

4. Energy Use and Conservation

It is important to understand that energy conservation practices have the best return on investment. When you analyze the cost to save a kilowatt of electricity, versus the cost to produce a kilowatt of electricity, conservation efforts come out on top. Efficiency is always less expensive than renewable energy generation until the point where you can't conserve any more energy, and the next best step is to start producing your own.

Reduce Consumption ⇨ Install Alternative Energy ⇨ Offset the Remainder

4.1 Lighting

Lighting consumes a big portion of the electricity used by the hospitality industry. Because lighting typically accounts for 10 to 15 percent of a hotel's total energy use, lighting efficiencies can result in significant cost savings. Improving your lighting can also enhance your ambiance and lighting quality within your business. Utility bills can represent a major cost so reductions in this area not only benefit profits, but many energy-use upgrades also improve guest comfort and satisfaction ratings.

Surveys have shown that hotel guests leave on more lights and leave them on longer than they would at home. They also use more water when traveling than they normally use at home. They don't pay the bills, so there is no cost implication. Efficient lighting technologies such as LEDs can reduce energy consumption from lighting by up to 80 percent compared to conventional, inefficient fluorescent tube lighting and incandescent bulbs that give off more heat energy that light energy.

Lighting technologies have drastically improved in the last 30 years, and today, the bulbs last far longer, reducing the frequency of replacements.

After good food, or a comfortable bed, almost nothing is more important to the guest experience than lighting in a restaurant or hotel room. Lighting helps set the mood because all humans are hardwired to react to light. We react both subliminally and with varying degrees of awareness when we focus on it; we react to the light's intensity and color temperature. All of this depends on the time of day and what natural light levels are occurring at the time. We have a tiny but important gland the size of a grain of rice in our brains called the pineal gland which reacts to the movement of the sun. All life on earth is subject in some way to this effect.

Warm light, which is how light appears from a lamp or candle, has longer wavelengths toward the red side of the color spectrum. This golden light triggers our digestive system. It also stimulates the production of the hormone melatonin, which creates the desire and ability for our system to rest.

Cool bluish-white light, especially if it is excessively bright, has the opposite reaction; this blue light feels like dawn to us and stimulates wakefulness. Cool blue or turquoise light and paint colors as well as very bright light can be an appetite suppressant decreasing our desire to enjoy food. Imagine trying to enjoy an evening dinner date in a room as brightly lit as a chain store pharmacy with intense bluish halogen lights overhead. Now think of a darker Italian trattoria with a wood-fire pizza oven and table candles with that same dinner date partner. This contrasted example shows how the same food served in those two environments would be received and enjoyed completely differently. We tend to enjoy eating supper in a room that has some darkness or lowered lighting levels, and we prefer golden tones of light for their effect on ambiance.

Color temperature for evening dining should be in the warm spectrum around 2,700 Kelvin or lower. In this range, you can buy energy-efficient LED bulbs in the Edison style that have an exposed glowing golden filament. These exposed filament bulbs have had a resurgence in popularity in hospitality environments because of this subliminal appetite stimulation effect.

Lighting at lunch is completely different, because at midday our natural clock expects and enjoys brighter light and makes us expect the sun to be overhead and at its brightest. When thinking about color temperature, lunch lighting should be in the 3,000-Kelvin range.

It is recommended that you have as much natural light as possible in rooms that serve lunch. This effect makes sunrooms, outdoor patios, and rooms with light that imitates sunlight, all very popular for lunch.

Ways to achieve enhanced natural light penetration may involve solar reflectors, clerestory windows, bay windows, skylights, and light pipes. Natural light can also be enhanced in your space simply by removing obstacles to daylight penetration (e.g., pruning trees and bushes that block windows).

Reflective surfaces can be used to amplify natural light such as mirrors, light-colored paint, and polished materials. Where natural light penetrates and what it might reflect can have major benefits when handled properly. Pay attention to flooring and ceiling colors as well as materials used in the furniture. Think of a billiard or ping pong ball bouncing and imagine those balls as photons of light bouncing through your space. Where do they enter? At what angle? Where will they bounce to if reflected and can those photons be encouraged to bounce or reflect more than once? This can be a fun exercise with good payback, moving a mirror or painting part of a wall might make a big difference to the lighting efficiency of your establishment.

LED lightbulbs and architectural LED lighting can range from general illumination to indirect lighting to slowly changing color washes now often used on exterior architectural lighting.

In restaurants, the kitchen will probably be the brightest lit area with specified light levels necessary for preparation and cooking. Minimum levels of light intensity (measured in lumens or foot-candles) are established and regulated by health departments. Although kitchen lighting does not consume as much energy as cooking, it is still worth considering new technologies that consume less energy.

You can reduce wasted lighting by installing motion sensors in areas such as coolers, freezers, restrooms, and storage areas.

Many utility companies offer grants that are available to operators who replace lighting and other energy-consuming fixtures and equipment with more efficient substitutions such as LED bulbs or Energy Star appliances. Look for opportunities to improve your savings with local government or utility subsidies before choosing your lighting models.

4.2 Equipment

Restaurant and hotel kitchens are high-traffic, high-output work zones where efficiency of planning, staff movements, and energy use are very important. While kitchens all have their processes and ways of operating, small changes can result in big savings. We encourage you to consider kitchen efficiencies as a potential profit area.

When designing or upgrading your kitchen, the first step is menu planning so that the kitchen has all the equipment and square footage that is needed, but no more than is needed to suit your menu. Functional efficiency in a kitchen starts with good planning. Designing the space to operate in a streamlined manner will reduce errors, improve workflow, and prevent wasted time and effort.

Integrating sustainability into a kitchen requires an analysis of the workflow of the kitchen such as, how do people move? Where is waste generated? When does the equipment get turned on? At what time must items defrost? Small behavior changes in a kitchen to reduce energy and water consumption, coupled with high-efficiency equipment will result in a kitchen with a smaller carbon footprint, and low utility bills.

Restaurants, compared to other businesses, are one of the most intensive energy users on a square-footage basis. They are intense because of the equipment in the restaurant (e.g., coolers, ovens, griddles, fryers, dishwashers, hot water heaters, exhaust hoods). These production zones draw a lot of power to store, process, wash, heat, chill, and change food. During prep times, food in the kitchen may be thawed or frozen, warmed or baked, churned, whipped, boiled, or broiled to get ready for food service, and all of this prep work consumes energy. As the customers' orders come in, the kitchen uses even more energy with food being finished for the table. With that in mind, simpler dishes, with fewer steps and processes, will inherently use less energy in your kitchen. This can also increase efficiency in your kitchen. Challenge the menu designer to consider ways to reduce steps without compromising quality of the food.

Equipment in your hospitality business may include the following list and more. As you purchase new equipment, aim to buy high-efficiency, Energy Star-rated appliances as your standard. Write this in a formal policy to ensure all purchasing decision-makers are on board and committed to energy reductions.

- Hot water heaters
- Exhaust systems
- Cooking equipment such as ovens, griddles, fryers, stove tops
- Refrigeration such as coolers, ice machines, fridges
- Dishwashers and glass sanitizers

- Laundry machines
- Air conditioners
- Coffee, soda, and snack vending machines

In hospitality businesses, energy is literally pouring out through exhaust vents as wasted heat. With building permit regulations, not only do we have to pay for the energy used by moving hot air, steam, and vapors through the exhaust canopy but we also now require make-up air which can be very energy intense. The air exhausted from the canopy over the cooking line has to be replaced and brought up to room temperature. On a winter day, this can represent a lot of thermal energy being consumed. The best exhaust systems today are heat activated so that the make-up air and hood vents are connected and they only operate as needed, unlike the old systems which ran at constant speed all day. The extra purchase cost can have short payback periods due to the energy savings.

Natural gas is preferred in most kitchens due to the speed of cooking but electrical induction is also catching on due to similar speed, performance, and easy cleanup. Buffet omelet stations in hotel banquet or function rooms are an excellent place for single-induction burners. As electric cooking and baking ovens get better, we will see more installations, such as at the Royal Bay Bakery in Colwood, British Columbia, which uses photovoltaic (PV) cells on its roof to supplement the power used in the bakery with eight to ten kWh of solar energy per day. This energy supplies power to the energy-efficient electric oven. The bakery also uses an electric delivery vehicle with a charging station connected to the building. Not only does this provide energy for baking and deliveries but the bakery received grants to offset some of the installation cost and it has received untold publicity benefits, making it a popular destination.

5. Heating, Ventilating, and Air Conditioning (HVAC) Systems

Heating, ventilating, and air conditioning (HVAC) is the stuff most of us don't see — essentially, it is the air system in your building. We can clearly see the water systems, and the lighting systems, but the air system churns in the ceilings, rooftops, and basements to keep our buildings fresh. You want fresh air that is at a comfortable room temperature. To get that, air needs to enter your building and be "conditioned" by filtering and warming/cooling. The stale air must be expelled through vents or forced exhausts that suck the air out of the space. The problem with inefficient HVAC systems is that they are constantly working to warm/cool new air, and expelling conditioned air. The energy input that goes into making your air comfortable can be massive. It is common for HVAC to consume 50 percent of a building's total energy use.

HVAC systems combine multiple forces to form another large consumption slice of the energy pie at your business. HVAC systems, when working properly, eliminate stale air yet retain warmth or cooling depending on the need at the time through efficient make-up air and heat recovery. Unfortunately, many HVAC systems in restaurants and hotels simply do not function properly. As space reconfigurations and part replacements occur over time, a system that was once effective may not be any longer. Whether you are newly constructing or looking for eco-retrofits to reduce energy consumption, it is important to look at your building, its envelope, and HVAC components as a system and optimize all air and energy flows.

Talk to an HVAC professional, and get to know your internal system and models of your current equipment. Have the professional show you a diagram of the airflow and how everything is working. Good control and smart system design should be the goal of every HVAC system in a building. Look for weaknesses and points of wastefulness in your system. For example, you may find that the exhaust fan in your kitchen is turned on at 5:00 a.m. when the janitors come in, yet the cooking doesn't start until 11:00 a.m. For six hours, your building will be expelling tons of warm, conditioned air, making the heating system work harder, for no reason. There is not yet any smoke and cooking air to expel. In kitchens, making sure exhaust systems are active when needed can create big savings in energy and dollars.

5.1 System considerations

Space conditioning is the term used for cooling or heating and moving fresh air through occupied spaces to make them comfortable for inhabitants, and it is a huge energy consumer. Each involves different energy-saving techniques. Make-up air intake replaces air that is expelled by exhaust. Ideally, make-up air is preheated by waste heat from inside the building (heat can be captured from hot water or air leaving the building). Using these heat exchangers on the outdoor air supply can significantly reduce energy consumption. Filter outside air as it enters the building to screen particulates and improve indoor air quality. Design systems to balance air coming in and air going out. Exhaust systems should not expel more conditioned air than is needed.

Pump systems can consume huge amounts of energy over time. Energy Star-rated components and smart system design can create significant savings and reduced energy use. If your pump system is inefficient or aging, plan to replace it with an efficient, smarter model.

5.2 Building envelope

To improve HVAC efficiency we must consider the building envelope. The windows, doors, walls, and roof structure insulate the building and keep your space conditioned to the right temperature. Your envelope, and how it operates, should become part of your HVAC system design. For example, if one room is gaining too much heat and constantly needing to be cooled, consider ways your envelope can naturally keep the room cool. Cooling can benefit from natural convection, heat pumps, Energy Star-rated air conditioning equipment and, most important, solar shading from the hottest solar angles. One old school technique is retractable awnings, which can often have the combined effect of shading your patio as well as cooling the interior. Modern architectural solar shading involves exterior solar baffles which also prevent excessive solar gain. Shading and insulation are "passive" methods meaning there are no moving parts or energy consumed to control the heat of your building. Making these methods part of your design can be effective and affordable in the long run. For more on passive designs, visit canphi.ca.

Although energy conservation through heating is easiest and most economical with improved insulation, meaning you need less heating energy for your space conditioning, your cooling also benefits from improved building insulation. This is most easily done in new construction, but whenever significant upgrades or renovations are planned, always consider insulation for your building envelope and better R value for your windows.

Because warm air rises, and cold air falls, the most important part of your building for insulation is the roof, so once you've paid for your heat, you may as well keep it as long as you can. Roof insulation and high reflectivity (or high albedo) roofing can have significant benefits. For example, white or light roofing like you see in the Bahamas reflects more light and heat than black roll-on membranes. The ice caps of the poles help cool the earth through this type of reflected heat.

Building envelopes represent an important factor in savings potential through lowered energy use because heating and cooling (space conditioning) uses the most energy in the hospitality sector. There are engineers and consultants who can assist you in assessing your facility that will help you determine how to make improvements.

5.3 Windows

Clerestory windows, light pipes, bay windows, bow windows, curtain walls, and even glass floors and railings, if done properly, will make good use of natural light. When windows and roof overhangs are designed to use sunlight penetration angles in different seasons, there can be amazing results in comfort, energy savings, and guest enjoyment.

For example, after almost three decades of restaurant design, JC's first restaurant project, The Teahouse in Stanley Park, in Vancouver, remains the best known, largely because of the careful use of glass. The greenhouse seating area at Swans Hotel in Victoria also gets excellent reviews because of its design. In both places, natural convection, rather than conventional air conditioning, is used to maintain comfort and air movement.

Window technology has evolved to offer a self-tinting option in bright sunlight similar to the sunglasses that adjust to various light levels. Glazing can have high reflectivity, and double and triple glazing can add R-value (an insulation rating) as can reflective film and coatings, which can make a difference to your windows and skylights. Check with local glazing experts about cost-effective opportunities to conserve energy.

Skylights are a green feature worth considering for your common areas, particularly if you serve lunch. Skylights can contribute to airflow by natural convection which saves energy while making your facility feel fresh, and the additional light allows you to save on electricity during the day.

6. Insulated Concrete and Structural Insulated Panels (SIPs)

Building science has responded to energy and resource challenges with significant developments. Two favorites are insulated concrete for wall panels and foundations and structural insulated panels (SIPs) in wood construction for walls, floors, ceilings, and roof structures. SIPs are Structural Insulated Panels so instead of solid concrete, for example, insulation is sandwiched with concrete to combine strength and insulation. Typical SIPs use rigid Styrofoam. However, Agriboard is a SIP that does not use Styrofoam; it uses compressed agricultural fiber such as wheat or rice straw, which are more sustainable because they are renewable and less toxic.

These developments are technical and your architect can explain how they work but the important point for this book is that new buildings can be built with significantly lower life-cycle energy consumption and with a much smaller carbon footprint than conventional buildings.

An example of an energy-efficient building is the Visitor Centre and Discovery Hall at the VanDusen Botanical Gardens in Vancouver, British Columbia. It is certified as a Living Building, which means it generates all the energy it consumes, saves all the water it uses, and there are absolutely no toxic building materials in its construction.

5
Water Conservation

 The hospitality business uses a lot of water; for cooking, cleaning, dishwashing, laundering, filling pools, serving spa clients, and for serving to guests. Water used in hotels and other lodging businesses accounts for approximately 15 percent of the total water use in commercial and institutional facilities in the United States. Conserving freshwater resources is a growing concern for many of your customers, especially with advancing drought conditions in areas across North America. As fresh drinking water supplies diminish faster than they can replenish, or become polluted by business, residential, or industrial activity, water becomes increasingly scarce and is raising concern in many areas.

As basic economics will predict, scarcity causes a rise in costs. Across North America, water-use rates are increasing and some municipalities are introducing stormwater charges, which means hospitality businesses have to pay for both the water they consume and the water that runs off their properties into the stormwater drains. Business owners can expect that water-related utility costs will continue to increase, especially in areas where aging city infrastructure requires fees from residents and businesses to offset upgrades and improvement costs.

In hotels and restaurants, there are many ways to conserve water. Often, conservation efforts will also save energy because much of the water used is heated by natural gas or electricity. Saving hot water also means saving energy. Making a plan to reduce water use in your business is a smart way to hedge against changes in both water supply and rate increases. Most importantly, conserving water will relieve pressure on the natural resources that supply your business.

Benchmark your current water consumption by totaling your annual usage over the past two to three years. Using that information, set a goal for reduction in the next one or two years. In hotels and restaurants, a 10 to 20 percent reduction in water use is a reasonable target for the first year with some capital improvements and staff behavioral changes.

In restaurants, the kitchen is the area with the largest water use followed by restrooms for customers. In hotels, most of the water is used in bathrooms, followed by landscaping, laundry, and kitchen use. If you are focusing on one area first, restaurants should focus on kitchens, and hotels on restrooms. Those are the areas with the greatest opportunities to improve water efficiency.

Water is a vital resource for our businesses, our planet, and our society. There is plenty of room for improvement through conservation efforts to save water, energy, and costs. A proper assessment and action plan will help your business make smart decisions to implement changes in your workplace that will lower utility bills and reduce your environmental footprint.

1. Water Conservation Tips

Because of the large volume of water involved, commercial conservation can take minimal investments to realize serious savings. Don't allow your water bill to drain money from your profits. Many water-saving tips simply require a change in practice, while others require a financial investment that pays back over time. Regardless of your restaurant or kitchen size, you can find simple, low-cost steps to save water and money.

1.1 Buy Energy Star-qualified equipment

Energy Star was created in the early 1990s by the US government and the Environmental Protection Agency (EPA) to help people find products that improve energy and water efficiency and reduce energy consumption. By purchasing all new appliances as Energy Star-qualified equipment you will conserve water and reduce water bills over time. For example, many combi ovens, which serve as convection, steam, and combination cooking, are qualified by Energy Star because they do not use a water line, so use far less water than comparable machines.

Choose certified models when shopping for dishwashers, ice machines, steam cookers, and fridges. Energy Star models ensure equipment is using at least 10 percent less water and energy than conventional equipment — and many products reach a savings of 30 percent.

Also look for WaterSense labeled products such as faucets, showerheads, and toilets. These products are certified to be at least 20 percent more efficient than standard models.

Some equipment, such as wok stoves and dipper wells, continuously use and replace water, running constantly through the system. Use these only when needed, or consider replacing them with a system that consumes less water.

1.2 Install low-flow spray valves, faucets, and fixtures

One of the most cost-effective ways to save water is to install low-flow prerinse spray valves. In kitchens, the dish pits use a surprising amount of water. A low-flow spray valve will cost approximately $100, but it will save up to 80 percent of the water used at that sink station, resulting in big savings in both water and energy.

It's recommended to install low-flow sink aerators if your faucet flows above 1.5 gallons per minute. To determine the amount of water flowing from each faucet, open the faucet to full force and fill a measuring cup for ten seconds. Multiply the amount of water in the container by six to get the amount of water flow per minute. In regular sinks in both bathrooms and kitchens, retrofit faucets with low-flow aerators that use 1.5 gallons per minute or less.

In bathrooms, consider installing automatic faucets that shut off when not in use. Toilets are major water consumers in high-traffic restaurants and large hotels. The standard water consumption in older models was six gallons per flush. New ultra-low flow models consume only 10 to 25 percent of what the old models used. Verify that your toilets are low-flow by looking for a stamp or sticker that indicates the gallons per flush. Water-efficient and waterless urinals are also available. Upgrade to low-flow toilet models in all bathrooms that use the old six gallons per flush toilets. Some toilets can be retrofitted to become low flow by replacing the tank and some basic parts, rather that the whole unit.

For showers, install low-flow showerheads that use two gallons per minute or less. Again, in all areas where hot water is used, saving water means saving energy too!

To conserve water that is lost while waiting for hot water to come to the tap, design your restrooms with the water heater located as close to the point of use as possible. Also, make sure hot water tanks and all pipes are insulated.

For all water and energy-saving initiatives, check with your utility company for rebates and/or incentives that may be available for water-saving appliances or fixtures.

1.3 Repair leaks

Water leaks can be silent water consumers in your business, and they can go undetected for years. This wasteful expense is something to watch for by periodically checking equipment and monitoring usage to notice any spikes. When there is a visible leak, make the repair a priority. A small dribble from a kitchen faucet may not seem like a big deal during a busy shift, but if it's from the hot side of the faucet, heat energy is going down the drain as well as wasted water.

Similarly, toilets can "run" silently and constantly, resulting in wasted water. To detect leaks in toilets, add ten drops of food coloring into the tank. If the colored water enters the bowl after a little while without flushing, you have a leak. These leaks are usually simple and inexpensive to repair. Make it a routine to check for leaking toilets every four to six months.

1.4 Wash fully loaded dish racks

A commercial dishwasher uses exactly the same amount of water no matter how many dishes are in the rack. Making sure the racks are full will make the dishwasher more efficient with the water it is already programmed to use. Train staff to arrange and fill the dishwasher for optimal use.

Evaluate the wash formula and machine cycles for maximum water and energy efficiency. For example, you may need to reprogram the machines to eliminate a cycle. In a conveyor-type washer, make sure water flow stops when no dishes are in the washer; install a sensing arm to detect the presence of dishes. Use basins of water to presoak pots, pans, and utensils.

1.5 Avoid running water

It is much more efficient to install a three-compartment sink so your staff can scrape, wash, and rinse easier and with less water than doing it all in one sink under a constantly running stream of water.

It is common in many kitchens to thaw food under running water. This can waste hundreds of gallons each time it is done. Instead, move frozen foods to the refrigerator to thaw.

1.6 Reuse gray water

Using gray water is one method of making the most out of your building's water usage. Any water that has been used in a restaurant or hotel, except water from toilets and urinals (black water), is called gray water. About 50 to 80 percent of wastewater comes from showers, sinks, and laundry.[1]

Treated water should be saved for drinking and bathing, but gray water may be reused for other purposes such as landscape irrigation. You can also use the excess water from steamers or other equipment to wash floors.

Many hotels in water-deprived regions are installing gray-water systems that filter, treat, and completely recycle the water from hand-washing sinks, showers, and rain.

1.7 Turn off water when not in use

Often, water is left flowing or machines operating when not needed in restaurant and hotel kitchens. Water conservation can be as simple as turning down a valve or turning off a switch.

Using pedal-operated foot controls for faucets at the dish station or hand sink can also help prevent water waste. Foot or knee pedals allow your staff to turn water on and off without contaminating their freshly washed hands, and they shut off automatically. Instead of using a hose to spray down kitchen floors and equipment, use janitorial supplies such as a mop and bucket.

1.8 Serve filtered water only when requested

Don't assume your guests want water. Instead, your servers shouldn't bring water to the customers unless they ask for it. It's worth noting that an 8-ounce water glass takes 16 ounces of water to clean. Alternatively, servers can pour excess water in pitchers from tables into planters on the patio.

---

1 "Gray Water Recycling," Environmentally Friendly Hotels, accessed August 2015. http://environmentallyfriendlyhotels.com/gray-water.php

Avoid serving bottled water because it is a needless expense and plastic bottles will add to your waste stream.

1.9 Compost food waste and conserve your landscape

Some areas in North America now mandate commercial food composting, with more districts implementing bans on food scraps in their landfills every year. You'll be a step ahead if you implement a compost program in your restaurant or hotel kitchen now.

Most hospitality businesses not only use water inside the building but outside as well. Follow water conservation best practices for your region and you may be able to use your own compost as nutrients for your landscape.

Consider xeriscaping; using site-specific, low-maintenance plants with mulch to keep soil moist and reduce water runoff. Water your landscape only when needed and early in the morning or in the evening when wind and evaporation are lowest. Install a rain-sensor device or other automatic shutoff device on irrigation systems and adjust the irrigation schedule for seasonal changes. Consider using low-volume irrigation, such as a drip system. Make sure irrigation systems are directing water to landscape areas and not to parking lots, sidewalks, or other paved areas.

1.10 Laundry

Some hospitality businesses launder in-house, while others outsource the service. In both cases, you can take action to conserve water, energy, and costs. It is common practice for hotels to leave instructions in their bathrooms asking guests to avoid requesting clean towels and sheets on a daily basis. This reduces laundry costs and has huge savings on water. Another benefit is the increased lifespan of sheets, pillowcases, towels, and cloths. These linen and towel reuse programs can reduce laundry loads by 17 percent.[2]

If your business outsources laundry services, ask your supplier about its sustainability practices such as type of detergents used, type of vehicle used for deliveries, water and energy conservation practices, and temperature used for washing. If you make sustainability key criteria in how you choose a vendor, your business will be encouraging your supply chain to adopt sustainable practices.

If your business launders in-house, consider options to reuse water from rinse systems for the first wash of the next cycle, which will

2 "Water Management and Responsibility in Hotels," Green Hotelier, accessed October 2015. www.greenhotelier.org/know-how-guides/water-management-and-responsibility-in-hotels/

reduce overall water use. Wash with full loads, using cold water and a detergent brand that won't pollute your water systems.

2. Pools and Spas

One of the mainstays of the hospitality industry has traditionally been the swimming pool, now updated to include spas, hot tubs, saunas, and other water-related recreational facilities. Whenever these facilities are being planned or upgraded, specific attention should be paid to water efficiency, energy conservation, and the life cycle of materials and equipment.

When constructing a pool, it is important to source high-quality materials because pools and their equipment can be very difficult to maintain if your surfaces and equipment are not designed for long-term durability. When built well, pools can last for decades with only minor upgrades, and they provide relaxation and exercise for your guests.

One of the best devices for water retention is pool covers. Evaporation is the primary source of water loss in pools and hot tubs. That water loss is almost eliminated during hours that pool or tub covers are in place. Covers also retain heat, which results in significant energy savings by using them at night when ambient air temperatures are lowest. Pools are a great place to consider solar hot water or even photovoltaic energy.

Another source of evaporative heat loss is the popular "vanishing edge" or infinity pools; although very attractive, these cause extra evaporation which in turn requires more energy to heat the replacement water and the pool which is naturally cooled by the evaporation process.

Darker pools attract more solar energy and may be appropriate where heating is an issue. Lighter colored pools attract less energy and will stay cooler in very hot climates.

The chemicals used to treat pools can also be harmful to local ecosystems when the water is released. An alternative to the traditional chlorine system is salt-water pools. There is chlorine in salt and the natural process of chlorine being released by adding natural salt to pool water allows for safe swimming with very low salt levels, about one-tenth the salinity of sea water.[3] Pools can combine a salt-water system with solar hot water and a heat pump for maximum efficiency and cost savings.

---

3 "This Summer Use Sustainable Swimming Pools," Sustainability for All, accessed October 2015. www.activesustainability.com/summer-sustainable-swimming-pools

6
Waste Management

Worldwide, restaurants and hotels are a major contributor to landfills. Most disturbing is the fact that most of the waste coming from restaurants is food. Businesses also generate large quantities of plastic, metal, and glass waste. While some waste is difficult to avoid, in many cities it is possible to create next-to-zero waste with proper purchasing, food processing practices, and disposal. Reducing waste will require everyone in your business to be on the same page. This is critical and also the most challenging part of greening a hospitality business, which is often plagued with high turnover due to seasonal workers.

However, with great challenges come great rewards. Our surveys found that businesses with zero-waste programs had a higher level of staff satisfaction. This was mostly due to the connection the employees felt with their place of work. They were proud to be working somewhere that made a difference. Many people today cringe at the sight of wasted food and heaps of garbage loaded with recyclable materials.

1. Conduct a Waste Audit

A waste audit is a report that details the type and quantity of waste generated at your business in a given week. We suggest conducting an initial waste audit to benchmark your performance and use as a comparison at a later date. When you have implemented some changes, you can conduct a second waste audit see how your business has improved.

To get started, the baseline audit will help you determine how much waste your workplace is creating and where it is coming from. Your baseline should include two key metrics:

- The total volume of waste you are creating. You can measure this in volume (gallons or liters) using bin sizes and how full they typically are when emptied.

- The weight of waste in pounds or kilograms. Ask your waste supplier if it is able to give you a history of the weight of your trash collection. Some companies track this internally and can produce reports fairly easily.

Note that weight is usually a more accurate measure than volume, and it is easily converted to a total carbon footprint if you would like to use that as an additional metric. The Nature Conservancy has a free online carbon calculator that you can use: www.nature.org/greenliving/carboncalculator.

Table 6 provides you with a chart to help you calculate your waste for your business. Table 7 provides you with a chart for your waste bin audit.

Once you understand the composition of each waste bin, you can determine where you need bins for organics and recycling. The total percentage of recycling versus organics and garbage will tell you what size each bin should be.

Your waste management company, local municipality, or an environmental consulting firm may offer a more in-depth audit, which could determine the total weights and composition of each waste stream. Contact your local providers to find out what kind of information is available. See Sample 4.

Table 6
Waste Management

Metric	Unit	Your Business
Total waste per month/year	Pounds, tonnes, kilograms OR gallons, liters, cubic feet	
Total carbon footprint from waste	Tonnes CO_2e (carbon dioxide equivalent)	
Diversion rate (recycled or compost waste diverted from trash)	Percentage of total waste (weight of recycling and composting divided by weight of total waste)	
Waste reduction	Total waste compared to previous year (percentage reduced)	
Waste intensity	Total volume of waste divided by revenue of the restaurant or total guests	

Table 7
Waste Bin Audit

Location:	Location:
Bin Size (gallon/liters/volume):	Bin Size (gallon/liters/volume):
Fill Frequency:	Fill Frequency:
Non-Recyclable Contents: Approximate %_____	Non-Recyclable Contents: Approximate %_____
Recyclable Contents: Approximate %_____	Recyclable Contents: Approximate %_____
Organic Contents: Approximate %_____	Organic Contents: Approximate %_____

Waste Reduction Comparison

Restaurant	Before	After	Result
Total Waste	100 kg/week	67 kg/week	33% reduction
Diversion Rate*	40%	75%	87.5% improvement

*Diversion rate is the total percentage of waste recycled or composted (diverted from landfill).

2. Food Waste

"Food waste arguably causes a significant financial loss for the entire industry; with improved management, this loss can be substantively decreased. Indeed, with operating profit margins falling to 4.2% in 2011 (Statistics Canada, 2011), the financial benefit of reducing food waste is apparent."[1]

— Sylvain Charlebois
Supply-Based Food Waste in the Food Service Industry:
The case of Delish Restaurants

According to a policy brief issued in 2008 by the Food and Agriculture Organization of the United Nations, close to half of all food produced is wasted in transit, at grocery stores, and in our kitchens. The authors state that the food crisis we may face is not one of production, but one of waste. The policy brief asks governments to reduce food waste by half, by 2025.[2] Food waste is increased as the steps to process and ship the food increase.

A study of University of Arizona states the percentage of food waste coming from fast-food restaurants is about 9.55 percent and in full-service restaurants it is 3.11 percent of the total amount of purchased food.[3]

When considering the cost of food is the second largest expense in the restaurant industry after labor, the argument for reducing food waste becomes very compelling. Reducing food waste in your restaurant by 5 to 10 percent can have a substantial impact on gross margins.

---

1 "Supply-Based Food Waste in the Food Service Industry: The case of Delish Restaurants," Sylvain Charlebois, accessed August 2015. www.ifama.org/files/conf/papers/959.pdf

2 "Saving Water: From Field to Fork — Curbing Losses and Wastage in the Food Chain," J. Lundqvist, C. de Fraiture, and D. Molden, SIWI Policy Brief, SIWI 2008, accessed August 2015. www.siwi.org/documents/Resources/Policy_Briefs/PB_From_Filed_to_Fork_2008.pdf

3 "Using Contemporary Archaeology and Applied Anthropology to Understand Food Loss in the American Food System," Timothy W. Jones, PhD, Bureau of Applied Research in Anthropology, University of Arizona, accessed August 2015. www.ce.cmu.edu/~gdrg/readings/2006/12/19/Jones_UsingContemporaryArchaeologyAndAppliedAnthropologyToUnderstandFoodLossInAmericanFoodSystem.pdf

Tackling food waste in restaurants is worthwhile, but it is not without its challenges. It is often noted that on-site storage and government regulations are among the many barriers restaurants face in reducing waste.

2.1 Imperfect foods

A trending concern is the amount of food that is discarded due to slight imperfections in shape, skin texture, color, or minor bruises. Failure to meet rigid quality inspections means this perfectly edible and equally nutritious food is used for feed, dumped, or tilled back into the soil. Many people will reject an apple for not having the perfect "apple" shape. These strict aesthetic screens prevent us from eating much of the food that yields from crops, wasting precious soil, water, and energy inputs. A grocer in Australia called Harris Farm Markets has reacted to this issue, launching the Imperfect Picks Campaign, which is designed to reduce food waste by selling "ugly" fruit and vegetables that might otherwise have been rejected.[4]

Similarly, a French supermarket called Intermarché aims to change our perspective on misshapen fruit and vegetables by a campaign launched in 2014 with a mission to end food waste. The third largest supermarket chain in France, Intermarché, is no small player, and its Inglorious Fruits and Vegetables campaign has turned the tables, celebrating imperfections in food that still has quality nutrition. The campaign features posters of unattractive produce with witty slogans: "Ugly Carrot: In a Soup, Who Cares?" and "A Hideous Orange: Makes Beautiful Juice."

Working directly with your supply chain, your business can specifically request imperfect produce, which can often be purchased at a far lower cost than its perfect counterparts. This is just one of the many benefits of farm-to-table, direct-supply relationships.

Here are some imperfect food solutions:

- Asparagus "seconds" are often skinny or stumpy asparagus spears. The unique characteristics could add a farm-feel to a plate; when pureed in a dish such as risotto, the asparagus shape is irrelevant.

- Apples that are too small or a slightly different shape are still fantastic in pies or fresh juices.

- Misshapen carrots or onions still make a great stew.

---

4 "Harris Farm Markets Grocer launches 'Imperfect Picks' Campaign," Sophie Langley (September 15, 2014), *Australian Food News (AFN)*, accessed August 2015. http://ausfoodnews.com.au/2014/09/15/harris-farm-markets-grocer-launches-imperfect-picks-campaign.html

Offering healthy, yet imperfect, fruits and vegetables can also help make quality, nutritious food more affordable. To combat food waste, enhance food security and affordability, we need to make room for the imperfect yields in our restaurants and grocery stores.

3. Reducing Waste from Your Suppliers

When we think of waste management, our first thought is to recycle and compost the waste we deal with, but the best first step is to look at reducing the waste that comes into your business from suppliers.

It is integral to the success of a hospitality business to have strong supplier relationships. Quality products, consistent supply, timely delivery, price-point, and adequate volume of products are all key considerations in choosing vendors. Recently, more criteria have been added to the list: Hospitality businesses are looking for vendors who can help them attain their sustainability goals — local supply and waste reduction.

The following are some key questions to ask your suppliers:

- Do you have any internal sustainability programs?
- How do you determine your vendors?
- Do you choose to supply local, green products?
- What options to do you have for products with reduced and/or compostable packaging?
- Do you have a program to combine orders to reduce deliveries and greenhouse-gas emissions?

To reduce waste, choose products that come with less or no packaging such as beer kegs instead of bottles. Mini-kegs for house wine are also becoming more popular in restaurants. Look at your purchasing list and cut unnecessary items such as frilly plastic-topped toothpicks, plastic garnishes, and ramekins for holding condiments.

Pre-cycling also implies choosing products that are packaged in more recyclable material such as items packed in cardboard rather than unrecyclable plastic, or products shipped in reusable containers.

Tip: Straws

A bar, café, restaurant, or fast-food joint goes through an incredible amount of disposable straws. Especially in cocktail lounges, or anywhere with a high-end bar, the bartender will typically use a straw to sample each drink before it is served. Hundreds and hundreds of plastic straws go into the trash every night. One fine dining restaurant in Victoria recently switched to metal straws for the bartender to taste each cocktail.

Alternatives to cheap plastic straws include:

- No straws (best option).
- Compostable straws (make available, but refrain from serving with every drink as these are more costly).
- Metal or paper straws (adds a unique element to the drink which can be favorable).

---

4. Revise Your Menu

The menu plays a role in waste elimination. Large menus with a breadth of options require more preparation and can result in higher food waste, especially for unpopular items. Consider cutting items that are ordered less frequently, especially if they require unique ingredients that are not used in other dishes. This will help avoid over-prepping foods that have a low-probability of being fully sold. Large menus require large inventories, which is another added cost and potential source of waste.

Design a menu with a balance of diversity; however, consider the ability to recycle components into other dishes or use them in a breakfast menu the next day. Often, chefs will combine leftover food components to make specialty dishes or soup stocks. Management should encourage and give incentives to the kitchen staff to utilize food items as best as possible and consistently reassess the menu to remove high-waste items.

Portion size is another consideration. Restaurants that offer "half size" options can realize higher margins while reducing food waste and the cost of packaging leftovers to go. The cost of the packaging coupled with the extra step in labor can eat away at margins.

Take a look at the food items that you use as garnish on your dish. This year we conducted a food study for a local restaurant to determine a strategy to move to a more sustainable food supply without adding too much cost. We cataloged how much the restaurant spent on each food item and found that cantaloupe was the second highest cost on the list. Thousands of dollars were spent on cantaloupe even though many customers left it on the plate at the end of a meal. This surprised the owners and they began to look for alternative fruits that would be eaten, would cost less, and could be grown closer to home.

The garnish can be an overlooked cost and source of food waste that doesn't add much value to a plate.

Tip: Whipping Cream

Aerosol spray whipping cream canisters are comprised of various metals and plastics, making them difficult to recycle. Often, they end up in landfills and sometimes in scrap-metal bins. Instead of using aerosol cans, your business can switch to whipping cream dispensers which typically cost $30 to $90 each. The steel cartridges contain N_2O, which is a greenhouse gas, but the small cartridges are completely recyclable.

Making your own whipping cream gives it a notably fresher taste. You also have the ability to flavor whipping creams with mint, orange, lavender, vanilla — whatever suits your dish.

---

5. Reduce Kitchen Waste

Simple practices in the kitchen can reduce food waste. Using appropriate peeling knives and other tools can reduce wasted product. For example, a good knife can cut a steak precisely without wasting any meat.

Food storage, rotation, and labeling are simple processes that will make sure your food products are used in the correct order and before they expire. Make sure all kitchen staff are aware of storage, rotation, and labeling protocols and include this in the training/orientation process of new staff. One idea is to store all new foods on one side of the fridge and have existing food moved closer to the other side. Have a sign that states "take from this side" to ensure food is used in the correct order.

6. Customer Waste

The communication process between guests, servers, and kitchen staff is important for reducing food costs and waste. Consistent communication and good work flow will reduce mistakes in food orders, which often mean tossed food. For example, burgers are automatically topped with mayo; should the menu and/ or the server not communicate this to the guest who does not want mayo, the burger will need to be remade.

In a study of Canadian restaurants, Sylvain Charlebois found "Waste also occurs when staff misread their orders, or when they lack concentration while they are working … Proactive strategies undertaken before waste occurs are more effective. These strategies groom a team to be more effective, which is the goal of a chef. Proactive strategies can be included through more rigorous line checks, accountability for waste, and constant staff training."[5]

Case Study: Zero Waste Restaurant in Chicago

"I'm not just going to do it half; I'm going to do it all the way."

— Justin Vrany, owner of Sandwich Me In, Chicago.

This Chicago establishment has become famous for its achievement in becoming a zero-waste restaurant. Vrany states, "In a typical restaurant about eight gallons of garbage is thrown out every hour. We did that in two years." His restaurant has a full composting and recycling program and he has adjusted the kitchen practices and supply chain to reduce waste as much as possible.

When customers come in and you get that immediate reaction, it makes me know that the passion I have for this is working and it gets me through the daily grind."[6]

6.1 Cafeterias and buffets

Studies have shown that food waste in cafeterias and buffets is higher than in sit-down or fast-food restaurants. In buffets, customers are free to fill their plates, often aiming to get their "money's worth" with less concern about the food that will be wasted.

In addition, health regulations often require that buffet or cafeteria restaurants throw away food items once they have been sitting for a certain period of time. Because items are usually mass-prepared, the kitchen waste compounded by the customer waste creates massive amounts of disposed food.

Some college cafeterias are addressing food waste by simply eliminating trays. Students are less likely to pile on excessive food if it becomes burdensome to carry. Instead, they fill a plate with a more reasonable amount they can eat.

5 "Supply-Based Food Waste in the Food Service Industry: The case of Delish Restaurants," Sylvain Charlebois, accessed August 2015. www.ifama.org/files/conf/papers/959.pdf
6 "How One Chicago Restaurant Went Totally Trash-Free," NationSwell, accessed August 2015. https://www.youtube.com/watch?v=uwg6ei2V6-4#t=102

7. Waste Management and Disposal

Effective waste management requires good communication and a well-organized sorting system. The following sections will give you some tips for proper waste disposal.

7.1 Fryer oil

Fryer oil in restaurants can be used to create biodiesel or other products such as animal feed. In communities where biodiesel producers will pick up from restaurants, they will often supply a drum or pail. These can be commercial producers, or small-scale backyard producers. Biodiesel is a carbon-neutral fuel that can be used in diesel engines, replacing fossil fuel consumption.

On Vancouver Island, a local company called Greasecycle picks up used fryer oil from restaurants and converts that waste to biofuel, which is then distributed at a local pump to members of their co-op.

7.2 Waste hauler

You will need to work with your local waste-management service provider to optimize your system and include as many streams of recycling as possible. Find out what services are available to your business and what items can be recycled. If your main service provider cannot recycle all of the waste streams you create, you may need to use a combination of service providers that can take different types of waste. More services results in more monthly costs, so it is important to make sure you are reducing your volume of waste as much as possible.

The following are some recycling items to consider:

- Compost/organics
- Paper and cardboard
- Metal
- Glass
- Cartons and paper cups
- Foil bags and wrappers
- Styrofoam
- Batteries
- Ink toners and cartridges
- Electronics
- Lightbulbs

- Hard plastics
- Soft plastics

Note that hard plastics are those numbered one through seven. If you are unsure, look for the number in the recycling symbol on the product.

Soft plastics, such as bags and food wrap, are more challenging to recycle. They are typically a lower grade product and can take more energy to recycle into a new product than rigid plastics. Wherever possible, it is best to avoid using excess soft plastics.

Ask your recycling provider the following questions:

- What items are accepted?
- How should materials be sorted?
- What organic compost items are not accepted?
- Are there alternative recycling options available in this area for the items you don't accept?
- How are the waste streams processed and what new products do they become?

7.3 Organize your bin system

When you organize your bin system, it is very important to have visual, easy-to-read signage with as few words as possible. Ideally, a person could glance at the sign and understand, in a split-second, what should go into that bin. Color-coded bins can help streamline your waste system and add another visual sorting cue (e.g., green for organics, black/gray for trash, and blue for recycling). Make sure to place bins at locations where the waste is created to reduce the effort people have to make to dispose of something.

A good rule of thumb is if the trash bin is available, it will be used. Trash bins should be small and sparsely available, only in areas where waste is created that cannot be recycled or composted.

7.4 Composting

Having an organics/composting bin will significantly reduce the amount of waste being sent to the trash. Options for composting at your business will depend on your building type and the services available in your region. Many cities have private composting pick-up services available. Some composting services even pick up using bicycle-powered trailers!

Fruit flies and odor are two common concerns with composting. Remember, the same material was entering your trash bin so there is not much different about the waste you are creating. However, there are a few ways to mitigate odors and flies. First, a compost bin with a carbon filter built into the lid will absorb odors. Make sure the bin is scheduled to be removed on a frequent basis (e.g., every one to three days, to avoid the sour smell that results from natural decomposition). To keep flies at bay, make sure your compost bin seals airtight when the lid is closed. Keeping fruit stored in a container or refrigerator instead of on counters will keep flies from reproducing. Adding cardboard to your compost will also help mask and contain any odors that occur due to the decomposition.

For easy emptying, you may choose to use compostable bags in your bin. Make sure the bags are "compostable" and not just "degradable," as degradable bags may still be made of plastic. Look for a bag that is made from corn starch or another type of compostable, plant-based material.

7
Furnishing and Finishes

When furnishing a hotel or restaurant, the options are endless and most decisions are based on cost and design. Furniture; mattresses; and finishes such as paint, wall hangings, flooring, and fixtures all have embedded carbon emissions, energy, water, labor, materials, and chemicals that were used in manufacturing and transportation. Consider the life cycle of your furniture:

- Where is your furniture from?
- Was the product made with sustainably sourced and/or green-certified materials?
- Were upcycled components used in the making of the product?
- Do you know what chemicals are in your upholstery and cushions? Do those chemicals emit toxins into the air?
- Is the furniture repairable if one part wears out or breaks; what is the longevity of it?
- Are the components recyclable at the end of its life?

With so much furniture being made overseas and sold at prices well below those of goods made in North America, it can be difficult to justify buying locally made furniture. However, life cycle cost-benefit analysis leads to a broader view of the value of a well-made local product over time.

One of the obvious problems with restaurant and hotel furniture is the heavy use and wear and tear over time. Durability is a key factor, as is repairability. In British Columbia, several hospitality furniture makers design products that outperform imported goods while supporting the local economy.

Learning to address maintenance and replacement problems, particularly with respect to furnishings, is an extremely important part of our industry. When buying a product, consider the long term. If you choose to purchase quality goods that are sustainable and can be obtained and repaired or replaced quickly and locally, you have made a better investment for the future. In the end, this will also mean less furniture in landfills.

Remember that every piece of furniture has an embedded carbon footprint such as the metal in the screws, the wood, paint, rubber, plastic, marble, glass, and all other components were harvested from natural resources. Not to mention all of the shipping emissions for transporting components and finished products over wide spans of distance. In our grandparents' generation, furniture items were lifetime pieces. Now, furniture lives a short life, filling our dumpsters and continually costing us money.

Case Study: Holiday Park Resort

Holiday Park in the Okanagan region of British Columbia includes 117 condos and 570 RV sites (leasehold and rentals), all fully serviced and landscaped. The resort hosts a multitude of recreation facilities such as four pools and three hot tubs.

The resort replaced all plastic pool furniture with wooden furniture. If the furniture breaks, it is fixed in the resort's little hobby shop on-site, instead of being thrown out or replaced every two to three years.

Holiday Park has great initiatives to save water, reduce energy consumption, recycle, and compost. The yard waste is converted to fertilizer to use on-site, and residents enjoy the garden plots and herb gardens. The resort has received numerous awards such as the Lake Country Environmental Award and the Kelowna Mayor's Environmental Award. For more information about this resort, go to https://sweetlife.com.

Many of the decisions and recommendations around furnishings will come from a hospitality business's interior designer. When contracting a designer, specify that you are looking for cost-effective and sustainable alternatives in furniture and finishing choices.

By having local manufacturers build your furnishings, problems such as repairs, replacements, and warranty issues can be dealt with much more promptly. Also, by selecting local furniture, a regional style can develop such as the West Coast eco look, urban bistro, New England traditional, and Quebec rustic. These styles all have regional character and are based on a tradition of local materials and vernacular style.

To make local style or the topic of regionally appropriate furnishings more understandable, imagine being in France on a patio on a Parisian bistro chair that perfectly suits that use, that mood, and that style. Similarly, Italian bistros have slightly different but inherently Italian chairs. In North America we tend to copy European furniture but there is an emergence of North American style, most notable being the mid-century modern style, much of which is being reissued or never went out of the catalogs of fabricators such as Herman Miller. An American classic bistro and patio chair resurging is the durable Navy Chair, now made with recycled materials such as pop bottles and recycled aluminum.

1. Furniture Materials

Not long ago, plastics had a strong presence in the restaurant business. Today the use of plastic furniture is largely confined to fast-food restaurants, outdoor patios, and sidewalk cafés. Within restaurants there has been a strong resurgence of wood for both chairs and tabletops. Wood chairs can be fabricated with a shaped wood frame which is a great way to create a product that rarely needs maintenance and when damaged can be repaired without need for a complete replacement.

Upholstered elements show wear first, so avoid padded armrests and backrests as much as possible. One of the most pernicious materials used in hospitality furnishings, particularly in seat cushions and fabrics, are fire retardants, most of which are carcinogenic and volatile organic compounds (VOCs). For seats, eco leather is a good choice because it does not require fire retardants, it has excellent durability, and it is generally resistant to spills. Natural, fire-retardant wool and latex are also good choices because they don't require chemical fire retardants.

For tables, plastic laminate may seem to be a good selection until it fails. We've all seen laminate tables with chipped edges or a worn pattern. These problems are almost impossible to repair and complete replacement is often the standard solution. Also, plastic has VOCs and laminate tops are often set with potentially toxic glues onto fiberboard tops which can have inherently high levels of formaldehyde. For many years, that was the standard with a hardwood edge being the upgrade option for durability.

Compare that laminate over Medium Density Fiberboard (MDF) to a solid oak tabletop that no matter what damage it suffers can easily be repaired, often by your own maintenance staff if it has an eco-oil-based finish as opposed to a factory finish with polymerized plastics or epoxy. Water-based lacquer finishes are acceptable but must be thoroughly off-gassed (i.e., gasses removed from material) before delivery.

The environmental aspect of chairs or seating extends beyond the materials, local sourcing, toxicity issues, and all the standard sustainability guideposts; ergonomics is important to your patrons for their health and comfort. It should also be important to you as an operator or owner because comfort is largely subliminal, but it will be part of customers' decision process when deciding whether to return to your facility. Chairs can be good or bad for posture, and for back comfort. Never buy chairs until you sit in a sample. Look for long commercial-use warranties, reinforced joints and corners, as well as eco-certification such as Forest Stewardship Council (FSC) wood.

Guest room furnishings can be an important green initiative; although price considerations have driven a lot of business offshore, we all need to consider what importing has done to regional economies, and if we pay attention to the shift toward local purchasing and sourcing, we actually keep more money within our own communities that can have positive benefits.

By purchasing beds, bedding, and soft goods that are eco-certified, flooring that is GreenGuard certified, with furnishings and case goods that meet the Sustainable Furnishings Council criteria, you should have guest rooms that you can be proud of without having to personally check the provenance and material specifications of everything that goes into your rooms.

1.1 Sustainable Furnishings Council (SFC)

The Sustainable Furnishings Council (SFC) is a nonprofit organization that promotes information sharing within the furnishings industry and practices that reduce environmental harm. Its mandate is that sustainable, environmentally safe, and eco-friendly furnishings are made and distributed in ways that protect our planet.

SFC members commit to minimize carbon emissions, to reduce waste-stream pollutants, and to avoid unrecyclable content. The SFC offers its members advice on waste recovery and recycling, energy-use reduction, health and environmental safety, and material choices. The SFC (www.sustainablefurnishings.org) has videos, seminars, and support for those who want to learn more about sustainable furnishings.

Restaurants and hotels can look for SFC certification as well as furnishing manufacturers that are listed on the EcoLabel Index (www.ecolabelindex.com).

2. Millwork

Millwork is important to consider because the materials sourced and used in typical case goods often have toxins such as formaldehyde in the finished products. They also have other volatile organic compounds (VOCs) which can have a combined effect on indoor air quality. Look for GreenGuard eco-certified products and materials, which do not have formaldehyde or toxic VOCs.

The International Living Future Institute publishes a Materials Red List, which will help you find the latest in eco-friendly materials while avoiding harmful ones (http://living-future.org/topic/materials-red-list).

3. Flooring

When considering indoor air quality and the health of your staff and guests, few areas represent the choice between good and bad, healthy and toxic, as the choices for flooring. Formaldehyde, toluene, polyvinylchloride, and other carcinogens abound. Install only GreenGuard-certified flooring in rooms in which people will sleep, especially if the windows don't open.

There are many ecological flooring options, for example, bamboo flooring. According to the authors of another Self-Counsel Press Green Series book, *Greening Your Home*, "Bamboo flooring is more ecologically beneficial to grow than hardwood. Moso bamboo is the most commonly used bamboo for flooring. It can grow up to four feet in 24 hours. It requires no irrigation in its native habitat and sequesters up to 70 percent more carbon each year than a hardwood forest."

Marmoleum is also a resilient eco-flooring made from cork, linseed oil, and mineral pigments on a jute backing. Marmoleum was installed at the University of Victoria Student Union Building in the multipurpose room where it has stood up perfectly to more than 25 years of heavy use without any need for replacement.

4. Paint and Wall Coverings

Paint and wall coverings are getting better in terms of green ratings, but similar to commercial flooring, this is a field where petrochemicals and volatile organic compounds (VOC) abound.

The paint company Farrow & Ball, and the wall-covering company Phillip Jeffries, source healthy materials for walls. Do your research to find low VOC paints and suppliers that use GreenGuard-certified wallpaper.

8
How to Green Your
Guest Accommodations

Hospitality businesses are expanding to offer a range of services in virtually every possible destination. Reaching every corner of the globe, from dense cities to the edge of civilization, hospitality is everywhere and still growing.

The sector has also stretched the typical business model to include many value-added services. Beyond the room and continental breakfast, many hotels and resorts have some combination of spa treatments, fitness centers, restaurants, cafés, smoothie bars, gift shops, tours, sports facilities, attractions, galleries, movie theaters, and vehicle rentals. The amenities of a hotel can be the key to helping your business stand out from the others. Increasingly, unique and unusual services are being added to the hospitality experience. Some hotels are integrating local culture into a hotel stay, with amenities such as dance classes and artists in residence.

As the eco-conscious and inspired traveler segment grows, we are seeing both in-room and value-added offerings with an environmental edge. The Basecamp Explorer Hotel in Spitsbergen, Norway, is set in the Arctic Archipelago; the staff educates visitors about one of the most fragile ecosystems on the planet, at the edge of human civilization. At this hotel you can learn to mush on dogsled tours across frozen fjords and glaciers.

Unique eco-experiences and amenities are becoming popular across every type of hospitality experience, from the truly rustic to the most luxurious. Your hotel rooms and the experiences provided are opportunities to bring progressive environmental practices in-house, and make a statement about your company's values and vision for the future.

1. Gift Shop

An attractive gift shop in your business will add a stream of revenue, but it is also a way for guests to experience local and culturally important products. Many gift shops display cheap magnets, mugs made overseas with corporate logos, and overpriced standard-brand toiletries that you can buy in any other general store. These gift shops are uninspiring. They lack distinct products and waste an opportunity to connect with your guests by offering something memorable.

A gift shop should curate a selection of merchandise that inspires and intrigues guests. Consider a regional sampling of product that is salient to the history of your location.

I visited the gift shop of an award-winning luxury eco-resort in Costa Rica where the goods visibly mirrored the corporate values. It was clear that the goods throughout the shop were carefully chosen for their social and environmental aspects. The windows displayed locally made clothing and bags from a woman's cooperative, traditional foods such as plantain chips, and goods made of recycled materials such as wood picture frames made from fallen trees and wallets constructed of recycled candy wrappers. Many of the products included information about the history of the components and why they are important to the region. Portions of the sales from the coffee and chocolate went to a rainforest conservation fund. Economically, many artists and small-scale, local makers benefited from this shop. The sales supported their small ventures and livelihoods.

If you have a gift shop in your business, consider a collection of sustainable products that are locally made, fairly traded, and benefit the local community and environment. Your gift shop is an extension of your business's values so if your focus is gastronomy, environmental tours, sustainable urban living, agriculture, or nature, have the gift shop reflect those elements. Guests will appreciate the unique and thoughtful assortment of goods and will take home something they feel good about purchasing. The following are some gift shop product ideas:

- Water bottles and reusable coffee mugs to help guests reduce waste.
- Reusable bags made from recycled materials.
- Local food products that support environmental or social causes.
- Artwork and creative products from local makers.
- Postcards made from recycled paper products.
- Walking and biking maps of your area.
- Solar phone chargers.
- Books written by local authors.
- Sustainable toiletries with less packaging that are locally made, green certified, and organic.
- Offer compostable or recycled bags instead of new plastic ones.
- Consider having a part of the gift shop dedicated to renting items that encourage active transportation such as cycling gear, running shoes, and umbrellas. This will enable guests who are unprepared to walk, run, or cycle to see your city without a vehicle.

2. Guest Rooms

In guest rooms there are many opportunities to reduce environmental impact. The earlier initiatives in green hotel rooms included water-saving showerheads and reduced linen changes to save both energy and water. Rooms can be designed or retrofitted over time to improve environmental performance. Consider a five-year plan with staged renovations that increase the efficiency and environmental aspects of your rooms. If you plan to implement the cost-saving actions with short payback periods first, you can use those savings to fund future improvements that have a longer payback time.

These are the top cost-saving green actions:

- Switch lightbulbs to LED.
- Install low-flow showerheads.
- Install low-flow aerators on faucets.
- Install dimmers on light switches.
- Reduce linen services.

- Offer bulk toiletries in dispensers.

These are some additional green actions you can take with more investment:

- Retrofit rooms with a new key-card system (there are new energy management systems that only activate energy systems in a room when the guest has entered via key-card).
- Install efficient heating and cooling systems.
- Use low-flow toilets.
- Use eco-friendly bedding.

In every aspect of a guest room, there are opportunities to reduce energy, waste, and water consumption and supply products with less environmental impact. Take a tour of one of your rooms and look closely at the details:

- How can you change your in-room products to reduce environmental impact?
- Can you switch to products that will reduce your utility costs?
- What aspects of the room will be memorable to the guest and share your values as a hotel?

For bathrooms, consider the following:

- Choose a toilet paper brand with Forest Stewardship Council (FSC) certified paper source and/or high post-consumer recycled content.
- Install energy-efficient hair dryers.
- Use shower curtains that are not made of PVC (polyvinyl chloride) plastics; these are known to off-gas volatile organic compounds. Instead, choose a natural fiber or recycled plastic.
- Install dispensers for shampoo, conditioner, hand soaps, and body soaps. This is becoming more commonplace, even in high-end resorts. This will significantly reduce plastic and soap product waste.
- Choose an eco-friendly soap brand that does not contain harmful toxins such as parabens and sodium lauryl sulphate.
- Provide shower caps that are eco-friendly. Brands such as Hydrea are made with PEVA plastic (a better alternative) and come in different colors and patterns.

For closets, consider the following:

- Provide energy-efficient electric irons such as those that are Energy Star certified.
- Supply hangers made of bamboo, recycled plastic, or another recycled material. Refurbish and repair old hangers and buy a durable brand that doesn't become disposable in a short time frame. You can have hangers made with recycled wood, or even laser-cut pressed cardboard for a modern look. Making recycled hangers could be a great project for a classroom, staff activity, or community group.
- Provide recycled or repurposed cloth bags (potentially from used linens) for laundry and information about green-laundering practices on the bags. Use detergents that are eco-friendly and wash in cold water, with high-efficiency machines.
- Re-stain or refurbish old luggage racks as they wear out. For new luggage racks, the simple construction also lends well to using recycled materials, such as old seat belts or rope and recycled wood.

For in-room kitchens, consider the following:

- Avoid single-use, disposable products such as plastic wrappers, plastic stir sticks, and single-serving creamers whenever possible.
- Choose a coffee machine that will keep waste low. The single-serving "pods" that have become popular recently generate a lot of plastic and metal waste that cannot be recycled because of the coffee inside the pod.
- Provide glass and ceramic reusable cups instead of plastic for in-room beverages.
- Avoid bottled water in the mini-bar, if possible. Encourage guests to drink tap water if it is safe.
- Install energy-efficient fridges in the smallest appropriate size. Check all fridges for leaking coolant on an annual basis. Coolants have a high greenhouse-gas emission effect when released into the atmosphere.
- Try something unique for your welcoming tray, such as polished recycled metal. Avoid cheap trays that will get nicked and scratched and will need replacement on a regular basis.
- Choose kettles that are energy-efficient and leave a note for guests to "only boil the amount of water they need." Kettles can be major energy consumers in a kitchen.

For the in-room workstations, consider the following:

- Provide notebooks or pads of paper made of 100 percent post-consumer material.
- Choose eco-friendly material for guest room book and binder covers, or reuse old covers. Include in the guest book information about "how to be an eco-friendly traveler," bicycle and walking maps, the hotel's environmental policy and values, and eco-tourism/volunteer opportunities in the local area for guests.
- Provide a desk lamp with energy-efficient LED lighting.
- Provide corporate pens with recycled metal, paper, or plastic content.
- Include in-room recycling bins for paper, plastics, metals, and all other recyclable materials.
- Provide newspapers upon request. Guests may be able to select the option for daily papers upon booking, choosing their preferred newspaper or magazine.

For bedrooms, consider the following:

- Provide wooden or repurposed tissue boxes with refillable tissue cartridges.
- Consider having live plants in the rooms to keep the air clean and increase the moisture in the air. Certain plants, such as pothos, are known to remove and absorb volatile organic compounds (VOCs) from the air.
- Provide organic cotton or bamboo bed and bath linens.
- Install ceiling fans in rooms to disperse warm air and/or naturally cool the room.
- Provide Energy Star TV and appliances.
- Include energy-efficient lighting throughout the room such as LED, or other highly efficient technology.
- Install blinds that encourage guests to use daylight and avoid unnecessary energy waste from lighting during the day.

If some of your staff are artistic, allow them to paint over the canvases of old paintings with a fresh new look. Choose a theme and color palette that suites the rooms and let your team use their creativity! This was done at the Parkside Hotel and Spa in Victoria, British Columbia, with great results.

Guest Room Energy Management Systems

Space heating in North American hotels can be the largest energy consumer in rooms. Guest Room Energy Management Systems are one of the latest developments in hotel energy management. The room key activates the room's energy systems such as lighting, heating, and ventilation. When the room is not in use, the system remains dormant to prevent wasted energy use.

Guests usually spend the majority of their time outside of their rooms, enjoying the surroundings. Energy-management keys can drastically reduce energy consumption from wasteful room conditioning. Designing this system to be a seamless transition requires careful planning and assessing typical occupant behavior in your hotel. While the results vary significantly depending on the hotel, case studies have shown that room energy-control systems have saved 10 to 25 percent in hotels in various regions.[1]

3. Janitorial Services

The janitorial routine can make or break an in-room sustainability program. It is important for the housekeeping team to have an in-room procedure that aligns with goals to reduce energy consumption and sort waste. A clear and outlined routine involving the following best practices will help reduce the environmental footprint of your accommodations:

- Turn off lights, coffee machines, TVs, fans, and other equipment.
- Open or close drapes and turn down heating/air conditioning in unoccupied rooms.
- Check for leaky air conditioning machines, faucets, and running toilets. If there are any problems, fix them as soon as you can.
- Sort recycling, organics, and landfill waste.
- Leave behind more toiletries for guests only when needed.
- Unplug equipment that "phantom loads" when not in use.
- Combine waste from receptacles into one bag when possible to avoid excessive plastic bag disposal.

---

1 "A Framework for Converting Hotel Guestroom Energy Management into ROI," Francois Carle, AJM Solutions Group,, accessed October 2015. www.ajmsolutionsgroup.com/pdf/A-Framework-for-Converting-Hotel-Guestroom-Energy-Management-into-ROI_US-final-revised.pdf

- Collect partially used shampoos and soaps and donate to charities such as Clean the World (www.cleantheworld.org) to remake soap for people in need.
- Clean with eco-friendly and biodegradable products.
- Use microfiber cloths instead of paper towels to save money and reduce paper use.

4. Common Areas

All hotels have common areas, even if it is only a check-in desk and lobby. Today many grand hotels have atriums, swimming pools, ballrooms, function rooms, breakout rooms, business centers, and patios. When we add resorts, the list of potential common areas includes everything from tennis courts to beaches and natural parks. How you operate within these common areas can say a lot about your brand and your green credentials. Extend your practices in your core operations to the common areas with considerations for environmental impact in each of the following areas.

4.1 Vending machines

Upgrade to machines with improved insulation and efficient cooling units. Be sure any existing units are not leaking coolants. Within the machines, install energy-efficient lighting and infrared sensors to turn on when a person is nearby.

4.2 Laundry services

For smaller hotels with in-house laundry services, utilize Energy Star washers and dryers that use less water and soap products. For white fabrics, use a non-chlorine bleach product that is less harmful on water ecosystems.

4.3 Hallway lighting and parking lots

Installing motion-sensor activated hallway and parking lot lighting will save significant amounts of energy. Rather than common area lighting being on 24/7, it will only be on when needed. This action can have a strong return on investment and short payback time.

4.4 Patios

Patios are another key feature of many hotels and restaurants. They are a place to dine, congregate as a group, and view the surroundings from an outdoor environment. The sidewalk café/patio is an integral part of Mediterranean and European culture and urban design, while in North

American design patio space is often not used because in car-centric cultures, patios have been forfeited to make more space for vehicles. Within the green movement, urban planning and hospitality development is reintroducing the common area and patio space, where the dominance of vehicles is subdued to construct a more human-centric experience.

This is important to the hotel and restaurant world, where eating and drinking on these patios is a growing trend. If you can add a patio to your hospitality business, consider the factors that will make it effective and sustainable — light and shade, wind and rain, heating and cooling. Patios also have a selling factor: When you see someone under an umbrella on the sidewalk, you know there is a food service facility close by.

You may be asking why patios are a green trend. Patios and the outdoor environment have a much smaller carbon footprint than buildings and the indoor environment. They can generate additional revenue, which can be used to further your green developments. What was once an unused roof or a sidewalk can become a revenue-generating space with less material inputs required to create the space. Even with glass windbreaks, retractable awnings, and landscaping, there is less embedded energy per customer than an indoor environment.

The following are some green patio actions you can use:

- Install electric infrared patio heaters (e.g., wall-mount or stand-alone models) rather than propane or natural gas heaters to keep your carbon footprint and costs low.

- Use patio heaters only when necessary. You can supply guests with blankets and shawls.

- Design your patio to be comfortable without the need for conditioning such as installing walls where winds can generate a cool breeze, utilizing natural shading from greenery, and using light paint colors to reflect light into dark spaces.

- Integrate plants and greenery that naturally help control heat. Consider native plants that will support wild birds and insects without the need for constant care and watering.

- Consider installing solar panels on top of sun-shaders to generate electricity in areas with high sun exposure.

- Capture rainwater from rooftop areas to irrigate patio planters.

- Utilize permeable stone pavers to allow water to seep into the ground water system, rather than creating runoff.

- For hard surfaces, consider repurposed wood, or boards of recycled plastic, rather than concrete or asphalt.
- Refurbish patio furniture or buy furniture that is highly durable and made from recycled materials.
- Utilize furniture cushions made from 100 percent recycled materials, such as ship sails or recycled upholstery. Commission a custom project using these materials as a feature for your patio.

4.5 Spas

Spas for beauty, relaxation, or wellness can all employ green practices. In spas, there is a strong synergy between environmental and personal well-being with the use of healthy and eco-friendly products. Look to implement a sustainable product policy at your spa to set the standard high.

The following are some green spa actions you can use:

- Choose environmentally friendly product lines without phosphates which can be harmful to water systems.
- Carry products with minimal, refillable, and recyclable packaging.
- Install low-flow fixtures for hair washing.
- Choose local products that are shipped over shorter distances.
- Use natural oils rather than petroleum-based candles, or LED candle alternatives with the "flicker" effect to reduce oil burning.
- Use eco-friendly towels, robes, and sheets made of organic fibers such as bamboo, cotton, or hemp.
- Choose infrared saunas, which are more energy efficient than steam or hot rock saunas.

4.6 Fitness centers

Fitness centers around the world are taking action to reduce their environmental impact with equipment that draws less energy, or even installing bicycles and treadmills that generate power for the building.

The following are some green fitness center actions you can do:

- Use cloths to wipe down machines, rather than paper towels.
- Consider not having TVs running 24/7 in the gym area. TVs could be activated by guests when desired.
- Utilize natural lighting and/or high-efficiency lighting.
- Install rubber mats made from recycled tires in workout areas.

- Employ self-powered machines such as bicycles, steppers, tread-mills, and weight machines that do not consume power.
- Consider installing machines that generate power for your building. You can reward guests for generating energy with a free beverage or special room perk to get them engaged in the idea of energy generation.
- Sell and/or lend out yoga mats made of recycled material.
- Provide tap or filtered water instead of bottled water.

5. Other Green Resources for Hotels

EnviroMedia Social Marketing and the University of Oregon's Green-washing Index is a great source of information for finding green products that speak to the values of your business. The index can be useful in determining green criteria or if a word such as "natural" on a product is simply a marketing device.

Another useful resource for hotels is the Ecolabel Index, which is a third-party environmental group similar to GreenGuard and Energy Star. The Ecolabel Index covers almost 460 international agencies which have set reasonable standards and established credibility within the global marketplace. The Ecolabel Index includes manufacturers from other countries.

Green Key Global, Leadership in Energy & Environmental Design (LEED), Leaders in Environmentally Accountable Foodservice (LEAF), and others have set standards which can be followed in many areas. You may want to explore the following list of eco-friendly organizations:

- Green hotel certification programs (www.ecogreenhotel.com/ecogreen-newsletter/EGH_Jan/green_certifications.html)
- Environmental Protection Agency's (EPA) Energy Star for Hospitality (www.epa.gov/region02/p2/hospitality/resources/energy.html)
- Green Key Global (greenkeyglobal.com/)
- Ecolabel Index and ECO Certification (www.ecolabelindex.com/ecolabel/eco-certification)
- US Green Building Council: LEED Certification (www.usgbc.org/leed)
- Environmental Management System (www.epa.gov/ems)
- EarthCheck Certification (earthcheck.org)
- Green Hotels Association (www.greenhotels.com)

- United Nations World Tourism Organization (www2.unwto.org)
- Tour Operators Initiative for Sustainable Tourism Development (www.toinitiative.org)
- Tourism for Tomorrow Awards (www.wttc.org/tourism-for-tomorrow-awards)
- The Travel Foundation (www.thetravelfoundation.org.uk)
- TripAdvisor GreenLeaders (www.tripadvisor.ca/GreenLeaders)
- Responsible Tourism Partnership (responsibletourismpartnership.org)
- Responsible Travel (www.responsibletravel.com)
- International Institute for Peace through Tourism (www.iipt.org)
- Green Travel Market (www.greentravelmarket.info)
- Fair Trade Resource Network (www.fairtraderesource.org)
- Inn at Laurel Point (www.laurelpoint.com)
- Clayoquot Wilderness Resort (www.wildretreat.com)

One of the most credible and internationally recognized sources of information is the Audubon Society (www.audoboninternational.org). It has a list of certified properties under its Green Lodging Program, which covers hotels, motels, resorts, inns, bed and breakfasts, and timeshares. Its guidelines are practical and its certification fees are reasonable.

9
Food

"What was once a source of fuel for everyone, and a source of solace and pleasure for many people, is now a vehicle for self-expression, a point of pride, a political statement, a declaration of identity and much more."

— Bret Thorn, Nation's Restaurant News[1]

Food is woven into our cultures, cities, personal sense of identity, and place in society. Food, and dining out in general, is a continually expanding and evolving trend, with more urbanites exploring the daily flavors offered by local restaurants. The "foodie" movement opened the doors of the world of gastronomy to the everyday person.

What you eat is a form of self-expression, and a statement. Are you adventurous? Health conscious? Moderate? Ethical? Consumers are seeing the food they choose to eat as an extension of themselves and their values. As people become more aware of issues related to industrial farming, environmental degradation, animal welfare, and climate

1 "Beyond Fuel: Modern Eating Linked to Identity, Community," Bret Thorn, Nation's Restaurant News, accessed October 2015. http://nrn.com/consumer-trends/beyond-fuel-modern-eating-linked-identity-community

change, they are attracted to places that share those values. Restaurants are now responding by engaging their customers in the story behind the food: Where it comes from, how it was raised, and prepared.

Most of our food in North America is now produced using large-scale crops and livestock operations. Industrialization was a step forward in yields of food production and a step backwards in long-term sustainability of our ecosystems. These industrial systems require fertilizers, pesticides, long-distance transportation, and other inputs that pollute waterways, soil, and the atmosphere. More sustainable agriculture practices tend to be closer to your location, with practices that see the farm and all its components as a system. Crops are rotated to feed the soil with nutrients rather than using heavy chemical fertilizers; livestock grazes the land and their waste is used to fertilize the soil. Healthy farm systems mean healthy local environments where humanity and nature can coexist.

1. Why Buy Local?

Many factors have led to the recent emergence of local movements around the world. One of those factors was the economic meltdown in 2008. The recession triggered people to look within their local communities for products and services, to become more resilient. The local movement is generating the popularity, and a combination of factors dominated by new economic models and increased food awareness are at the forefront of this important social change. Your restaurant can benefit in several ways with a well-considered approach.

David C. Korten is an economist and bestselling author who has been at the forefront of the movement to support local economics. Korten champions a Main Street versus Wall Street concept. Helping to found the Business Alliance for Local Living Economics (BALLE), a local business promotion organization with chapters in many cities and regions, Korten's basic premise is that local people working with a local economic focus are less likely to make choices that could harm their community economically, socially, or environmentally.

The international movement for slow food is being promoted as an alternative to fast food. It encourages people to preserve regional and traditional cuisine as well as farm plants and livestock that are from the local ecosystem. There are various international initiatives around food from local markets to slow food-certified towns in Italy, where the slow food movement began, to towns in North America like the slow movement-certified town of Cowichan Bay on Vancouver Island.

On south Vancouver Island, the Island Chefs Collaborative, the Food Eco District, and local farmers' markets such as the Moss Street Market are changing the food delivery model. The Island Chefs Collaborative is a small group of chefs who decided to agree to support local organic growers for the mutual benefit of the local farmers and restaurants. They worked to build relationships with farmers and stabilize the organic and local supply chain which local consumers now enjoy. This sort of initiative and many similar local food movements elsewhere are enhancing the food-security model all across North America.

Victoria now has a growing list of producers and makers of wine and cheese, growers and farmers of organic meats, and organic fruits and vegetables. There is also the harvest of wild-caught fish and seafood. The relationships with the hospitality sector are vital to the survival of makers and farmers.

At the University of Waterloo, Ontario, the head chef of a $19 million dollar campus food-service organization goes market shopping at the local farmers' market three times a week and buys fresh fruit and produce for the campus where it is sold to students and staff from food carts at several convenient locations.

There are local economic movements of note in the Pacific Northwest; most notably Portland, Oregon has a program called "Supportland." This is a loyalty program that celebrates local business. Whatcom County, Washington, used a "buy local" campaign to shift the economics of the entire area; it evolved through good planning and marketing, which helped it go from one of the poorest counties in the US to one of the most successful counties per capita in about a decade.

Look into your own local economy because membership and participation in local campaigns can be good for your business, good for your community, and good for establishing a local food service. BALLE should be able to help identify groups and initiatives in your region.

If you shop locally for your food, produce, wine, and beer, then you will not only support your local economy and food-supply chain, but you will also benefit by promoting regional cuisine which can have a multiplier effect when enough restaurants, chefs, and suppliers participate. San Francisco is an example of this kind of movement through its cooperation with the Napa Valley and Mendocino County.

Sometimes a trend is a front-runner for a movement and there is every indication that what we are seeing today in local food production, regional cuisine, and farm-to-table will become the new reality, as a series of factors such as high-energy and transportation costs, climate change, and global security threaten the standard agri-business model.

Although there was pleasure taken from menu items such as exotic snails or rare wild plants flown halfway around the world for people's enjoyment in the 1990s, today the most celebrated chefs are wild-harvesting their local fields and forests and then letting their diners come to where the food is freshest.

Nowadays, several restaurants have their own herb gardens on the roofs or behind buildings. Shelter Restaurant in the surf village of Tofino, British Columbia, has its own herb and leaf garden because they are a long and winding road away from the farms of the island. Shelter Restaurant lists all of its food suppliers on the menu, with fish and seafood coming off the docks across the street and meats and produce coming from farms on the island and the nearby Fraser Valley. This trend is increasing, but Shelter Restaurant was the first restaurant on Vancouver Island to identify its food-supply chain.

The Piccino restaurant in the Dogpatch District of San Francisco has a farm-to-table policy with a buyer who nurtures personal and seasonal relationships between its producers and chefs, keeping the menu current and providing the best local produce.

Local food movements require cooperation and patience but the payoff can be enormous and the marketing costs shrink as awareness of your local region grows.

2. Wild, Edible Flowers

During my time in university, I was fortunate to be taught by Nancy J. Turner, a global thought leader in ethnobotany, the study of the relationships that exist between plants and people. She opened my eyes to the ways the First Nations communities survived off the land and how they understood the local ecosystems. Much of her research involved in-depth interviews with the elders of aboriginal communities to document their traditional uses, names, and perceptions of plants.

In Turner's book *Food Plants of Coastal First Peoples*, she suggests that building an economy around wild foods can serve to protect forested land. Instead of logging, the wild foods can be sustainably harvested from the same plot. Wild edibles can serve as non-timber forest product, developing small-scale yet profitable industries that do not remove standing trees, thereby preserving intact ecosystems. The hospitality sector can serve as a market for these wild foods which include mushrooms, berries, greens, seeds, nuts, roots, and herbs. As long as these wild foods are not overexploited, they can provide a sustainable, reproducing source for local restaurants.

Culturally, food is very important to us. It is at the heart of our socializations but we have lost connection to the food sources that grow wild near our communities. Your average restaurant plate includes starches, vegetables, and spices from other continents. Local, wild foods offer a deeper connection between the place we live and the food we eat. There are likely dozens of plants, flowers, mushrooms, vegetables, and fruits you weren't aware that you could eat that grow in a nearby lake, ocean, field, or wooded area.

Sooke Harbour House, a world-class resort hotel, spa, and restaurant located in Victoria, British Columbia, grows foods such as wild onion, salal, and Blue Camas, which are used in specialty dishes. It has an edible landscape on its grounds with more than 200 edible herbs, flowers, and vegetables. All of it is grown naturally, organically, and seasonally.

The following sections provide you with some examples of wild foods grown in North America.

2.1 Cattail

Cattail is almost impossible to misidentify. Also known as bulrush, these plants are usually found near the edge of freshwater wetlands. Cattails were a staple for many Native American First Peoples. The leaves, stem, and rootstock are edible.

To eat cattail raw, pull on a stalk and where it pulls from there will be an edible part to eat. You can even eat the young flower spike like corn on the cob. The pollen from the spikes can be used as flour in baking or cooking.

Location: Northern hemisphere

Season: Spring and fall

Use: Roots, stalks, flower spikes, pollen (used like flour)

Favorite recipe: Cattail Pollen Biscuits from Eat the Weeds (www.eattheweeds.com/cattails-a-survival-dinner)

2.2 Rosehips

The rosehip is the fruit of the rose. Rosehips contain a high percentage of Vitamin C (50 percent more than oranges) and offer a boost to our immune systems. They also contain a variety of antioxidants. Rosehip oil is used widely in natural cosmetics.

Location: North America, Asia, Europe

Season: Fall

Use: Boil in water and strain the hips (avoid consuming rosehip fibers because the insides have fine hairs that can irritate the digestive tract); serve rosehip liquid with hibiscus, and other herbals

Favorite recipe: Iced rosehip tea with raspberry leaves, hibiscus, and lemon

2.3 Miner's lettuce

The name miner's lettuce came from the Gold Rush when miners would eat this leafy vegetable that grew wild. The vitamin C available in the plant helped the workers avoid scurvy from malnutrition. Miner's lettuce tastes much like spinach and, like spinach, it can be eaten raw or cooked.

Location: Coastal and mountain regions of the United States, Canada, Mexico, Europe

Season: Spring

Use: Leaves, stems, and flowers

Favorite recipe: Miner's lettuce salad with roasted beets, arugula, baby beet greens, toasted walnuts, and blue cheese

2.4 Chicory

I was surprised to learn this woody plant is entirely edible. The pretty blue, purple, and white flowers are an impressive addition to a dish. Chicory is cultivated for its roots, flowers, and leaves. The flowers have been used in Germany in tonics to treat gallstones. Roasted and dried chicory root is used as a herbal substitute for coffee.

Location: Australia, New Zealand, North America, Europe

Season: Spring and summer

Use: Young leaves in salad, flowers eaten raw or blanched, root used in a variety of ways

Favorite recipe: Herbal espresso in Carolyn Herriot's *The Zero-Mile Diet Cookbook: Seasonal Recipes for Delicious Homegrown Food*

2.5 Chickweed

Common as ground coverage in gardens, chickweed forms a thick mat of edible leaves and flowers. The plant has small white flowers that are also edible. Chickweed connoisseurs serve the whole plant chopped and fried, in soups or raw in salads. Chickweed is high in vitamins and minerals such as niacin, potassium, beta-carotene, and zinc.

Location: North America, Eurasia, Greenland

Season: Spring

Use: Serve raw in a salad or cooked, as you would use spinach

Favorite recipe: Chickweed Pakoras from River Cottage (www.rivercottage.net/recipes/chickweed-pakoras)

2.6 Dandelion

Being the lawn's arch nemesis makes the dandelion an underappreciated herb. The entire plant is edible and has valuable medicinal properties. It is often used to aid digestion and treat infections. The flowers, leaves, and roots can all be consumed. Young leaves are great additions to salads.

Location: North America, Eurasia

Season: Spring and summer

Use: Leaves, roots, flowers

Favorite recipe: Warm spinach salad with blanched dandelion leaves, garnished with dandelion flower petals.

2.7 Fireweed

Fireweed has beautiful, edible purple flowers that have a peppery taste. The plant is a great source of vitamins A and C. The leaves and stalks are best eaten when they are young, before they become bitter. Fireweed honey is popular for its distinct, spiced flavor. Koporye Tea is a Russian tea made from the leaves of fireweed. The tea is not widely known in North America; however, in Russia it is recognized as a traditional drink with a wide variety of health properties.

Location: Northern hemisphere, abundant in open fields and forest areas

Season: Spring and summer

Use: Roots, leaves, stalks, and flowers

Favorite recipe: Dried leaves used to make tea with added fireweed honey.

Sustainable Wild-Food Harvesting

Some wild plants are endangered species and overharvesting can decimate a population. Familiarize yourself with the endangered plant species in your area and instead of harvesting them, plant seeds from the local wild species. Learn about sustainable harvesting techniques and only pick what you need. Make sure to leave enough in each patch to allow the plants to regrow.

If invasive edible species are present, focus on uses for these plant foods and harvest plenty to allow the native species to thrive again. Examples of these may include Himalayan Blackberry (Pacific Northwest region), Autumn berry (Maine, Alabama), Asian clams, watercress, and fennel. Do not collect plants in nature reserves or conservation lands.

Important: Do not eat anything you unless you can 100 percent identify it and know that it is safe.

2.8 Edible flowers

Sustainable agriculture can include flowers, which are a great addition to your arsenal of culinary ingredients. Many flower petals contain vitamins A and C as well as minerals. In addition, the pigments often contain powerful antioxidants. Add a splash of fresh colors such as pink, purple, and yellow to a dish.

Growing your culinary flower garden near your restaurant or on your hotel premises will be a beautiful point of interest for guests.

Consider using the following flowers in your culinary adventures:

- Rose petals
- Nasturtium

- Pansy
- Bergamot
- Violet
- Calendula (also called marigold)
- Cornflower
- Clover

3. Foraging

Wild-food foraging is a growing trend in culinary travel because more people want to dive, hunt, and forage for their dinner. These authentic, unique experiences offer more than a meal — they are an education. When you gather your dinner, you learn about where it comes from, what human impacts change its environment, and how it interacts with other species. You also learn how to harvest the food in a sustainable manner so as to leave more for the next harvester. Foraging also offers a connection to a primal state when humans used certain foods at specific times of the year, traded between populations, and entirely lived off the land.

Foraging is a seasonal sport, with different wild foods available at different times, but foraging can also be done at a farm. More restaurants are offering "forage and feast" experiences where guests can enter a nearby forest, field, or the restaurant's own vegetable garden and pick items for the dinner menu. Many foraging experiences end with a gourmet meal prepared by a seasoned and knowledgeable chef. This is an experience food connoisseurs love for the ability to explore the flora and fauna of a local area, all in the context of eating a great meal. A true foodie loves to know about how the food grows, when it can be harvested, and how it can be prepared.

A great example is the Hunter Gather Cook school in England, which specializes in foraging, outdoor living, and self-sufficiency. Visitors are immersed in the outdoors and learn life skills such as gathering mushrooms. Meals are had in the woods, and students learn about gathering spring greens, building clay ovens, home smoking, and wild cocktails.

4. Communicating to Guests

The theme of local and sustainable is more than a trend; it's a lifestyle and preference for those who are health-conscious, aware of environmental issues, and keen to support local economies.

More guests, especially those known as "neo-travelers," like to know more about the food they are eating and where it comes from. Give guests enough information to appreciate what they are eating and the life cycle of the food. These people like to get their hands dirty; they want the full story and the raw experience. They seek unique experiences, new cultures, and authenticity. To appeal to this growing group of diners, travelers, and locals, ingrain your sustainable sourcing and values into your overall brand.

Sales representatives, service staff, and chefs should be well-versed in the aspects of your sustainable menu and food sourcing. Make sure every employee has this information as part of their orientation and have easy-to-understand fact sheets available and visible to staff at all times. Your team is the face of your company, and every staff member should be able to answer questions regarding your sustainability program.

10
Employee Engagement

"Employee engagement is a workplace approach designed to ensure that employees are committed to their organisation's goals and values, motivated to contribute to organisational success, and are able at the same time to enhance their own sense of well-being."[1]

Campbell's Soup former CEO, Doug Conant, famously said, "To win in the marketplace you must first win in the workplace." Activating your workforce is key to the success of every business. An employee who *wants* to be there is the best employee. But what makes the person want to be there?

Deloitte's fourth annual Millennial Survey results showed that millennials believe businesses should focus more on people and purchase, not just products and profits.[2] These studies have shown that, especially for the millennials, working for a company that has strong environmental and social values leads to higher engagement and commitment from the workforce.

---

1 "What Is Employee Engagement?" Engage for Success, accessed August 2015. www.engageforsuccess.org/about/what-is-employee-engagement/
2 "The Deloitte Millennial Survey 2015," Deloitte, accessed August 2015. www2.deloitte.com/global/en/pages/about-deloitte/articles/millennialsurvey.html

It makes sense. If I believe in what my company does and how it operates, I'm going to put more into that company because it's more than a job, it's a way for me to do what I believe is right. A paycheck only goes so far to motivate people; beyond that, there must be meaning. We know now that many people will take pay cuts to work somewhere that exercises good values.

Researchers are uncovering the truth about what motivates us. Dan H. Pink, author of *Drive: The Surprising Truth about What Motivates Us* says we are not as predictable as you would think. Pink states that three things drive us: autonomy, mastery, and purpose. Autonomy is the urge to direct our own lives, mastery is the desire to get better and better at something that matters, and purpose is the yearning to do what we do in service to something larger than ourselves.

If a workplace is showing leadership and determination to make a difference, it will have a positive impact on overall morale and employees will have respect for the company they work for. Engaged employees lead to higher productivity and quality of service as well as to happier customers, generating customer loyalty and repeat sales, which is more profitable. It's worth it to invest in building a great culture, and sustainability can play a key part in your businesses values, culture, and reason for existing.

1. How to Get Your Staff Involved in Your Green Policies

Although values and awareness are shifting towards a mindset of sustainability, getting staff to change their behavior in areas such as recycling, purchasing, and energy efficiency can be a struggle. It is possible to shift the culture of your restaurant or hotel, but it will require patience and a plan.

1.1 Vision

Leadership should present a vision for your business to become more sustainable. Share what inspired this and ask for input on whether or not your people feel this is important. A strong vision and support from leadership will help chart the path forward.

1.2 Education

Educate your team on the environmental impacts of the hospitality business and connect the operation to local and global environmental issues.

1.3 Team

Form a green team that meets regularly to move sustainability actions forward and monitor progress. Even quarterly green-team meetings can maintain momentum towards the goal of becoming a sustainable establishment.

1.4 Action

Involve the staff, at least one member from every department, in creating a sustainability action plan for your business. You may want to conduct a baseline assessment of your operations through a third-party certification program, or outside consultants' advice and base your plan on the opportunities identified.

1.5 Results

Measure the results of your program and communicate them to the whole staff. You may want to measure total waste, energy consumption, and water consumption. Reinforce that their small changes are making a real impact.

1.6 Innovation

Foster innovation by creating open forums to discuss new ideas. Ask your staff questions and help them problem-solve to overcome obstacles on the way to reaching your goals and vision of a sustainable restaurant, hotel, resort, clubhouse, or whatever type of hospitality business you operate.

These steps will help jump-start a sustainability program and engage staff in co-creating a new standard for how the business will operate. To reinforce and maintain a culture of sustainability over time, consider the following points:

- Have a green champion team that regularly meets and reports in staff meetings.
- Integrate sustainability into training and orientation.
- Develop, with your team, a policy around sustainability for the company. Make it visual in the workplace where employees check-in every day.
- Continue to share inspiring stories from other businesses that are taking action on sustainability.
- Make your progress visible; set goals and update progress on a regular basis. Post the information in a staff room, somewhere visible for everyone to see.

- Provide your team with a sustainability course. You could offer a workshop, or a bursary for a local course.
- Get staff outside to participate in or learn about sustainability. Dedicate one afternoon per year, or even a lunch hour, to a beach clean, removal of invasive plants, tree planting, or other activity. Reward the team or person who makes the biggest impact.
- Make it easier for staff to use sustainable transportation to get to work (e.g., provide bicycle racks, or transit pass discounts).
- Have an online forum, white board, or another medium where staff can share ideas and notes about sustainability.
- Include environmental goals in annual and quarterly planning, and report on these to staff as you would financial metrics.
- Conduct annual sustainability surveys asking staff for feedback and suggestions. You can ask them what they are most proud of, and how they think the workplace can improve.

By providing inspired leadership, openness to new ideas, and encouragement for team effort and regular communication, your business will start to see a culture shift and an awareness of environmental and social sustainability in day-to-day operations. This will not only reduce your impact on the environment, but it will also create a better environment for your employees.

11
Guest Awareness and Engagement

"Leading businesses of the future will be those whose core business directly addresses global challenges."[1]

— World Business Council for Sustainable Development

 Globally, there is a growing middle class that is consuming clothing, food, and other daily-use products at a higher rate than a few decades ago. Companies and governments are faced with the challenge of changing consumer behavior by promoting a more sustainable lifestyle and product options.

Brands and local companies are in a position to help global consumption become more sustainable. Whether it is providing recyclable or reusable packaging, sourcing local and seasonal produce, or offering customers full warranties, all kinds of businesses can change how they empower their customer base to make a difference in their daily lives. Even clothing-care tags such as those used by Levi's include messages

---

1 "Sustainable Consumption Facts and Trends," World Business Council for Sustainable Development, accessed August 2015. www.saiplatform.org/uploads/Modules/Library/WBCSD_Sustainable_Consumption_web.pdf

for owners to encourage less impact on the planet. The tags advise consumers to "wash less, wash cold, line dry, and donate to Goodwill."

The world needs businesses to play a leadership role in shifting consumer patterns to a more sustainable lifestyle. Consider the ways your business can change its operations, educate your customers about sustainability, and engage them in meaningful experiences that enhance their understanding of the environment.

1. The Role of Hospitality Companies

Hospitality brands have a critical role to play in creating a dialogue and increasing awareness in the global population. Restaurant and accommodation brands are destinations; they are places where people connect and share ideas. They inspire their guests to try new experiences and new cuisines. They are the gateway to a city so they have an impact on visitors' perceptions of that place. Ultimately, restaurants and accommodations enrich people's lives and inspire the way they live and travel.

The following are some examples of how you can help make a change:

- Provide a more sustainable product or service.
- Help peer businesses become more sustainable.
- "Edit" supplies, which means removing unsustainable products from your supply list.
- Help consumers understand the impact of their purchasing power.
- Discover and alleviate barriers to sustainable lifestyle (e.g., install a bike rack).
- Share your story to inspire others and to build awareness.
- Reward your guests for being green (e.g., Crowne Plaza Copenhagen Towers offers free meal vouchers to guests who use its electricity-generating exercise bicycles).[2]

As an exercise, work with key employees to explore Figure 2. Brainstorm all the ways that your company could influence your supply chain, customers, and community to be more sustainable, enhance community well-being, and reduce environmental impact.

Servers or concierges may not identify themselves as potential agents for positive change, but they are. They become your ambassadors, your essential messengers of the company's brand, and what it

---

2 "The Pedal-Powered Hotel," Tom Robbins, *The Guardian*, accessed August 2015. www.theguardian.com/travel/2010/apr/14/hotel-with-electricity-generating-exercise-bikes

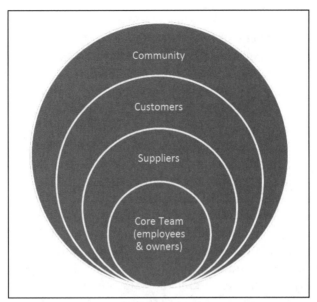

Figure 2: Hospitality Business: Sphere of Influence

stands for. Having well-educated staff is necessary if you are looking to educate and inspire customers. Explore options for staff to communicate key pieces of information to guests such as menu items and where they came from, the origin and values of the company, and the ways your business is tackling environmental issues. Integrate these lessons into your orientation and continued training programs and make the information readily accessible. Consider fact sheets, posters, regular memos, and other communication tools to keep the message of sustainability clear, current, and top of mind.

Business activities and communication can also educate policy makers. In developing new policies and regulations, the government often looks to leaders in an industry. By proving that the change is viable, leading businesses raise the standard for the whole industry. For example, a regulation to compost all food waste could come into place after a handful of businesses show that it is operationally possible. The government doesn't typically roll out a policy without any proof of it working in a way that doesn't completely disrupt business norms.

This speaks to the issue of leadership. While consumer behavior, government regulation, and commerce are all part of an intertwined system that must work together to create change, business arguably is in the best position to lead the charge. Businesses have resources and, most importantly, the risk-taking ability that lends well to pushing the sustainability movement forward.

Many hospitality businesses that have embarked on a sustainability journey have directly influenced the personal lifestyle of those who work for and visit the business. The journey builds awareness of how our everyday actions affect the planet and society. When a coffee shop in Victoria, British Columbia, publicized its mission to reduce waste and described its initiatives to recycle foil bags, soft plastics, Styrofoam, and cartons, the public became more aware of the ways to recycle these materials and started new bin systems in their own homes. In another example, a restaurant made a move to reduce wasteful straws. The restaurant publicized how many straws it went through in a year and shared its plans to reduce straw consumption in half. By sharing this, customers became aware of the vast amount of plastic that is used for only a few minutes and then wasted. This helped customers understand the changes, and many embraced the idea of "strawless" cocktails and appreciated the initiative on the part of the restaurant to take a stand on plastic waste.

Another major area of influence is the ability to educate and inspire peer businesses. Peer businesses are simply other businesses that are within your network. Maybe a nearby shop owner frequents your restaurant, or a group of business managers from another city stay in your hotel when they are in town. They may witness the changes to your business and, if you make the information available to them, they can understand your company's values and mission to become more sustainable. These peer businesses can glean interesting ideas, perspective, and proof that they can take back to their own companies, which helps them take action in their planning and daily business. Informing peer businesses raises the bar for your industry and helps to set new standards of practice. Most certifications or standards are created by a collective of businesses in a sector that is embracing a better way to do business. (See Figure 3.)

1.1 Educate

Educating your guests about sustainability is not only good for your brand, it is good for society. Guests can discover valuable information from the places they stay and dine. They can gain new perspectives, new information about the places they live or visit, and discover where their food comes from.

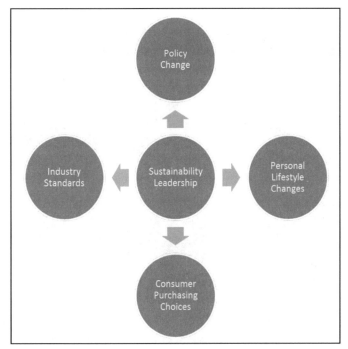

Figure 3: Impact of Sustainable Leadership

Tip: Use an infographic on the back of your menu, online and/or as a poster in-house to create a visual of your sustainability efforts and the impact they have had.

Whole Foods has been recognized for its educational campaigns. Its community blog shares recipes and tips on healthy eating for kids and showcases local products and farmers. Other companies use "how to" video series, Q&As with local suppliers, entertaining social media campaigns, poster displays, white papers, cooking classes, and even self-guided tours.

1.2 Empower

When you are confident your customers have a better understanding of sustainability, look at how your business could empower them to make a difference. In the narrative, you may explain how small changes in our daily lives can have a big impact.

Tip: Use a social-media campaign and unique hashtag to promote sustainable behavior and raise awareness about what your company is doing. An example is The Village breakfast restaurants, which switched to more local produce and got on the "food not lawns" bandwagon

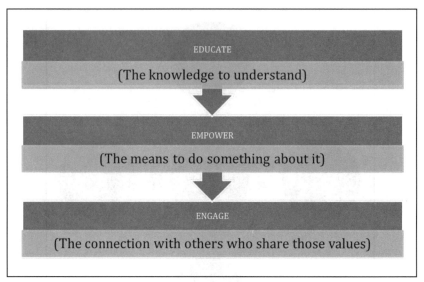

Figure 4: Process to educate, empower, and engage customers

to promote growing food in your backyard. The company created the hashtag #VILLAGEgrowshow for pictures of its own garden and other local produce.

1.3 Engage

Engaging your clientele is the final step to building a culture of sustainability throughout your customer base. In this stage, a customer can interact with others and be involved at a deeper level. This may include a foraging tour, an opportunity to volunteer, visit a farm, and attend a talk or a special event.

Tip: If you already have a decent social-media following, run a contest for the best concept to solve an environmental problem you have (e.g., a creative way to reuse a specific kind of waste). Get customers engaged in your business by letting them use their creativity.

The following are some additional tips to encourage your guests and employees to help your business stay green:

- Post a friendly reminder in rooms asking people to turn off lights when not in use. Also, some smart-wired hotels have key and desk-activated systems to save energy when the rooms are not in use.

- Implement a towel and sheet reuse program (e.g., change linens every three days unless otherwise requested by guests). Reward and thank guests who accept this program.

- Remind housekeeping staff to turn off lights and set temperatures to minimum levels after servicing rooms.
- Place refillable shampoo and soap dispensers in guest rooms, which will help eliminate small plastic bottles and excess soap packaging.
- Promote recycling by placing small recycling bins in guest rooms.
- Make sure you provide maintenance staff with a schedule to regularly check equipment to optimize performance and prevent energy losses as well as prolong equipment life.

By improving awareness of green issues and possibilities for positive change we begin the process. By engaging with staff and guests we create bonds between people and their communities that builds momentum for change while developing a more empowered and connected business.

12
Brand Recognition and Marketing

One thing we know about consumers is their decision-making process is complex. So what motivates a person to become loyal to your brand? It's a combination of consistent product, great service, and a shared set of values. Fortunately, for green restaurants, the consumer is becoming more conscious which presents an opportunity to integrate a narrative of sustainability into your company that will resonate with and inspire guests. A customer experiencing your business may be pleasantly surprised to see your proactive approach to environmental issues. That notion of responsibility and care for the community and the planet can establish a deeper sense of trust with your customer base. It may be why they decide to come back, to order another course, or recommend your place of business.

Making information about your environmental values and actions available to the public will strengthen your relationships with existing customers. They may already patronize your business, but there is value in enhancing their experience and giving them a reason to feel good about choosing your company over your competitors. It may be the reason they stick with you, instead of switching. It is difficult to measure the feel-good effect people get when they buy from a company that shares their values but we know it is a powerful motivator for customer loyalty and that is worth more than most advertising campaigns.

1. Sharing Your Story

The strongest brands today are offering their customers more than a product, they are offering them knowledge and empowering them to exercise their values, which are good reasons for integrating environmental information into your marketing.

Once your business has successfully measured and reduced environmental impact you may wonder, "How should we go about telling people we are green without boasting?" Or, "When will we have accomplished enough to start talking about being green?" The ideal time to promote your achievements is when you have results in the form of metrics or visual environmental changes to share. It is also valuable to share stories of the challenges your business overcame.

To do so, you need a succinct, compelling story or conversation to share. Start at the beginning — with your motive and reason for addressing sustainability. Consumers want to hear about what drives a company, just like they like to hear more about the significance of a dish, not just what's on the plate. Describe the major milestones on the journey to sustainability and what you have achieved thus far in relation to your goals. Finally, let people know what your future plans are and mention the next steps you have in mind.

The Village restaurants in Victoria did this well. It displays an infographic of its journey to carbon neutrality. Each milestone on the journey is represented with an icon, and the company shows customers how far along in the journey it has traveled. When it released the graphic on social media and with poster displays in the restaurants, it was on milestone two of five. Sharing progress gets the customers involved and the visual makes it easy to understand.

Displaying your story will also educate guests and give them a broader understanding of sustainability, which they may then choose to apply to their personal lives.

2. Marketing Tactics

Shape your brand to convey your values so they are incorporated into every aspect of your operations and communications, without being pushy or obnoxious. Use a variety of marketing tactics and media channels to integrate your values:

- Use social media to communicate changes in your workplace, and the results.
- Add a page to your website to make your green information accessible.
- Create posters with information to post in your lobby and restrooms.
- Apply for environmental business and/or innovation awards.
- Get certified as a green business.
- Engage the media by sending press releases and writing letters to the editor.
- Write blog posts on how you overcame challenges to go green.
- Include sustainability information in your flyers, pamphlets, and other materials.
- Publish a "Corporate Social Responsibility Report."
- Do speaking engagements for classrooms, peer businesses, and associations.

3. Greenwashing

You may not want to market your sustainability program because, simply, that's not why you are doing it. Maybe you think it's the right thing to do, and your business ethics don't need to come into play in your marketing. I would argue that this is a missed opportunity not just for your brand, but more so, for your ability to change the world. Your company could be setting an example for your guests, peer businesses, and competitors. Keeping your story in a vault restricts your ability to act as an agent for change.

For many businesses, their greatest fear is that they become seen as "greenwashers" for marketing their efforts. They have been annoyed with greenwashed products and services and have felt a sense of betrayal from a company or brand for its lack of honesty. The last thing they want is for their customers to feel that way towards them. For this reason, many companies engage in the opposite sin, termed "greenhushing." In this case, companies stay silent and don't discuss environmental performance whatsoever.

If you have this same concern, we encourage you, as we have with other companies, to tell the public what your business is doing to be more environmentally friendly in a transparent manner. Speak to the metrics, facts, and specific changes or results within your business. Avoid using blanket terms and statements such as, "we are sustainable." Tell the customer your values and what you do to work towards sustainability, and let them decide if you are sustainable or not.

Greenwashing has indeed increased consumer skepticism, but you can gain and maintain consumer confidence by communicating your environmental performance with transparency and clarity. The following principals will keep your business accountable and allow you to market your products or practices without greenwashing:

- **Be transparent**: Talk about the wins and the losses, your strengths and your weaknesses.

- **Be specific**: Speak to what your business has actually achieved. Avoid general terms such as "we are a green business" because consumers will ask, "What made you green?" What actions are backing this proclamation? What were the results? Do you have any numbers or metrics to show?

- **Be real**: Use the human element. Draw on the values of your company. Why did you decide to go green? What was your inspiration? What were the challenges?

- **Make it visual**: Paint a picture of what you are doing; use graphs, charts, and infographics, but keep them simple. Post the results where people can see and make it visually engaging.

First and foremost, marketing your efforts will have a positive impact on your brand and customer loyalty; companies have stated this was the greatest benefit to greening their businesses. Again, there is another reason to market your green efforts: You will be raising the bar for your industry and setting an example of responsible business practices.

13
Green Events

 The hospitality sector hosts a wide range of events, from conferences, to meetings, sports shows, weddings, parties, and corporate events. These occasions can be heavy consumers of natural resources, and they tend to produce a lot of waste. When you consider travel, food sources, purchasing, decor, and other factors, events are big opportunities to reduce your environmental footprint. Often, simple changes to planning and purchasing can have a big impact. The Environmental Protection Agency (EPA) has specifically noted marketing, hotel stays, food services, and exhibitions as major sources of waste generated from events such as meetings and conferences.

The notion of green events, small or large, is taking off. In 2012, the International Standards Organization (ISO) came out with ISO 20121:2012: "Event sustainability management systems — Requirements with Guidance for Use." The 2012 Olympic Games in London was the first major event to test-drive this standard. They achieved a "zero waste to landfill" games by designing color-coded bin systems for sorting, separating organics for composting, refurnishing items for reuse, and renting equipment instead of buying. The framework of a green event helped the Games minimize environmental impact and increase positive impacts for the local community. In turn, the London Olympics inspired other major events around the world to think about the local communities and the environment from start to finish. The Olympics have developed specific initiatives to determine how sports can promote positive action that strives towards sustainability.

The Academy Awards, FIFA World Cup soccer games, and even the Barenaked Ladies tours have all taken action to reduce the environmental footprint of their events by switching to renewable energy sources, reducing waste, improving recycling, and reducing printing.

Meetings and events are a multibillion-dollar industry in North America and there is certainly growing demand from customers to host events that consider environmental impact. Visibly greening an event is an opportunity to educate millions of people and demonstrate sustainability in action. Events can set the bar and encourage attendees to take those practices and ideas to their homes and workplaces. Sometimes it takes going to a Barenaked Ladies concert to learn about recycling — but hey — whatever works!

The *Green Meeting Guide 2009*, published by the United Nations Environmental Programme (UNEP), defines a green event as one that is "designed, organised and implemented in a way that minimises negative environmental impacts and leaves a positive legacy for the host community."[1] This is a strong definition because it also encapsulates the economic benefit of the event on the local economy. Events in our communities support small business through event services, and attendees usually patronize local restaurants and retail shops. Events are an opportunity to share what is special about your city, and create awareness about sustainability.

Events consume a lot of energy so here are a few actions to reduce impact:

- Supply efficient, LED lighting in the venue.
- Use dimmable settings to conserve energy and make use of natural light.
- Employ a generator with renewable fuel, such as biodiesel.
- Install low-flow aerators in sinks and low-flow toilets in restrooms.
- Reduce the need for heating and cooling with efficient systems and properly managed settings.

---

1 *Green Meeting Guide 2009*, United Nations Environmental Programme (UNEP), Sustainable United Nations, accessed August 2015. www.unep.org/sustainability/docs/Green MeetingGuide.pdf

Purchase green energy, or give guests the option to purchase green-energy certificates to offset energy use from an organization such as Bullfrog Power (www.bullfrogpower.com).

1. Food and Beverage

Creating the option for a green event can set your organization apart from the rest, and generate added value. When catering to weddings, private functions, or large groups, offer an option for a set menu based on local and sustainable ingredients.

Provide water, juice, and other beverages in pitchers or reusable containers, avoiding plastic water bottles. You can also encourage guests to take food home in containers if there is extra left over.

2. Guest Transportation

If your business is close to public transit options, help guests navigate the system and take advantage of low-emission transportation options. You can also provide safe route cycling maps, bicycle racks, and a bicycle tire-pump kit on-site to encourage cycling as a zero-emissions option. Car sharing and/or shuttling from an event will also reduce emissions.

3. Waste Management

If your restaurant acts as a vendor at farmers' markets or other events, consider the packaging you will be giving customers and the waste stations that will be available for the customers on-site. If you are supplying all-compostable packaging, be sure there is a compost receptacle in the vicinity. This may require working with the event manager and encouraging him or her to set up a comprehensive recycling and composting system. This, in turn, could encourage other vendors to also use all-compostable packaging for their food items.

Most events today still use an incredible amount of paper, but some are going completely paperless. Consider electronic communication with guests including for registration activities. For meetings, having an agenda on a whiteboard, projector screen, or flip chart visible to all will reduce printing and costs.

Having proper waste-sorting stations is critical at a green event. Appropriate procurement and recycling streams on-site will assure all products at your event are compostable and recyclable. Opt for signage with images and color-coded bins to make sorting as easy as possible.

4. Procurement

Those in charge of choosing products and services for the event should consider, from the outset, environmentally and socially responsible choices to make an event truly sustainable. Help your guests by providing a resource list of sustainable services and products they could source from your local area. Include businesses such as furniture rentals, audio visual, and recycling companies.

Point your wedding planners to green wedding and event guides such as *Green Bride Guide*, which has fabulous ideas for eco-friendly decor, invitations, flowers, and more.

Here are some creative decor ideas:

- Use poker chips or wooden tokens in place of paper drink tickets that get thrown away. The chips act as a currency for drinks or meals and can be used as a dollar value for different combinations. You can use them again for future events.

- Use LED solar lights instead of burning candles. You can even get ones that have a warm glow and flicker like a candle.

- Use chalkboard paint on old doors, recycled wood, or old framed paintings to make reusable event signage.

- Add some flair to the event by making pennant strings out of used wrapping paper, burlap, butcher paper, scrap fabric, or other recycled material.

- Use old corks or pinecones for name-card holders at weddings or dinner events. You can also use leaves and gold or black ink for name placements.

- Use fruits, greenery, and potted plants for centerpieces and decor.

5. Environmental Days

Environmental days are a great way to connect your business to a global movement. Through these events, your business can engage others from around the world in sharing ideas to make our communities greener and more integrated with our local and global ecology. Your business can take part by hosting special events on environmental days. The following are just a few of the many events you might want to celebrate in your business. For more environmental dates, visit www.PlanetFriendly.net.

National Environmental Education Week (Mid-April)

Held primarily in the United States, National Environmental Education Week (EE Week) is a celebration of environmental education "inspiring environmental learning and stewardship among K-12 students." (www.eeweek.org).

Earth Day (April 22)

Events worldwide are held to demonstrate support for protecting the environment. Earth Day was first celebrated in 1970, and is now hosted in almost 200 countries annually. It has been used as a platform for communities to announce new programs, policies, scholarships, and commitments to reducing environmental impact and moving forward as a progressive community. Earth Day is also celebrated to build awareness and take action on environmental causes that are salient to individual communities (www.earthday.org).

International Compost Awareness Week (First full week of May)

International Compost Awareness Week (ICAW) is a comprehensive educational initiative featuring composting. (compostingcouncil. org/icaw).

World Oceans Day (June 8)

World Oceans Day was originally proposed in 1992 by Canada at the Earth Summit in Rio de Janeiro, Brazil. It was officially recognized by the United Nations in 2008. Communities host educational events, beach cleans, fundraisers, and celebrations for protecting the world's oceans (www.worldoceansday.org).